Advent
Christmas

Proclamation 4

Aids for Interpreting
the Lessons of the Church Year

Advent
Christmas

Christopher R. Seitz

Series C

FORTRESS PRESS   PHILADELPHIA

Library of Congress Cataloging-in-Publication Data

Proclamation 4: aids for interpreting the lessons of the church
  year/Christopher R. Seitz.
     p. cm.
  Consists of 28 volumes in 3 series designated A, B, and C, which correspond to the cycles of the three year lectionary. Each series contains 8 basic volumes with the following titles: Advent/Christmas, Epiphany, Lent, Holy Week, Easter, Pentecost 1, Pentecost 2, and Pentecost 3.
     ISBN 0–8006–4153–1
     1. Bible—Liturgical lessons, English.   I. Seitz, Christopher R.
BS391.2.S37 1988
264'.34—dc19   88–10982

Printed in the United States of America   1-4153

95   94   93   92   91   2   3   4   5   6   7   8   9   10

Contents

The Advent Season

More than any other season in the Christian year, Advent calls for the worshiper to adopt a fresh temporal and existential perspective. Falling as it does after the long summer season of Pentecost, Advent asks us to look toward a rapidly approaching event, one that sets the Christian in an orientation point from which the entire drama of the Christian story will unfold.

But there is also a certain irony in what Advent expects of us. The irony, or mystery, of the Advent season is that we look forward with mounting expectation to a near-future event: the birth of the Christ child, the irruption of the Kingdom of God, and the dawn of a New Age. Yet these are events that have already occurred at a specific moment in past history. In order to see these events as future and imminent, we must adopt the perspective of scriptural texts, in which the nature of God's intentions for Israel, the church, and the world are sketched out, as lying in a future ripe with promises about to be fulfilled.

But the irony is only partial. It is clear in the texts themselves that the significance of the Christ event has not been exhausted by historical fulfillment, regardless of the temporal perspective of the reader. In the power of the Holy Spirit and through conscious participation in the liturgical reenactment of these saving events, we stand again on the brink of something spectacular, with the power to shatter our limited human expectations about ourselves, our neighbors, our world, and our God. From the perspective of these ancient texts, God's action in Christ is more than a matter of soaring rhetoric or the deepest yearnings of the human heart, though these factors do shape the way the story is told. An event actually had to take place, at God's own initiative, within the plane of human experience and understanding. The texts state that this event occurred in rough conformity with what was expected and longed for, but also as an explosion of the expected.

The nature of the text's own presentation forces us year after year to go back to Bethlehem. Thanks to the shape and power of these canonical texts, which demand our participation in their world and, in this instance, their advent expectation, we are catapulted back into a world and a circumstance not our own in order to have that world and that circumstance author our present existence before God. As such, we are able like those at the manger to worship and give praise not from a distance, but from a proximity provoked by our awareness of the full impact of the Christ event in the biblical story, in the history of faith, and in our own personal lives.

Historical criticism of biblical texts has taught us that in purely developmental terms, the earliest New Testament proclamation about Jesus involved not Advent or Christmas, but Easter events. Spiraling out from the crucial events of death and resurrection, further traditions coalesced about the birth, teaching, and full mission of Jesus of Nazareth. The Gospel genre was conceived.

Advent allows us to participate in texts that speak of Jesus at his earliest earthly moment. This is their brilliant gift to us. We cannot be sure in any sense that temporal or geographical proximity to Jesus was an aid to faith or discipleship (John 20:29). If this is true of the adult life and ministry of Jesus, it is all the more true of his lowly birth in Bethlehem. It is only as a result of the mature reflection of the post-Easter church that we have access to the full significance of that birth within the Gospels. Now, at the beginning of Luke's story, we are granted eyes to see in its full radiance the nature of what God was doing. Our distance from these first events is no more a hindrance for us at our twentieth-century vantage point than it was for the first Christians. Faith in the one whom God raised from the dead opens our eyes to that child in the crib, enabling us to gaze in awe and wonder with the eyes of first witnesses. Through the vehicle of the biblical witness, with all its rich expectation, we are empowered to go to Bethlehem and worship the child who becomes the terrifying king. We glimpse the power of our God expressed in fragility and risk. Yet at the same time, in that same child, the whole story—the powerful presence in teaching and healing, the risk of compassion and truth, the road to Jerusalem, to Golgotha, and to Emmaus—lies before us, waiting to unfold. That story involves the child becoming a man and the man showing himself in essential coordination with the One God who sent him and who promised his appearing. Like the texts that tell of his advent, we arrive relatively late on the scene. But we arrive with the knowledge of the full story, and the impact it has had in history and in the drama of our individual lives. And so we go to Bethlehem again, to stand again with first witnesses and hear of promises being kept, promises that have to do with who he was and who we are and why we are.

But before we hear of the birth we hear of much else in the Advent season. This is clearly a time of preparation. It is right and proper that we begin the season well into the story of Luke (chap. 21) with texts that speak of the second advent of Christ. There was a long period of preparation for that first advent, and we hear of it within the New Testament account as having to do with very old promises still fresh for a new hearing and a final denouement. But the second advent, we are told, will come without warning. What we know for sure is that the Christ who is to come will be the same Christ who has already come, but in full glory and majesty, where eyes of faith will recognize what they have longed to behold. While we cannot know the hour, we can know the agent. And indeed, with no sure timetable, and with the promise of tribulation and the struggle for faith, we are left with this one demand in all its sharpest relief. We must, then, go back to Bethlehem to see the One with whom we have to do, that knowing him we might be set in proper stance before him. May this Advent season prepare us to meet the One who has come, who continues to address the believer with that first advent appearance and who promises to return without warning but with full power and majesty and everlasting dominion.

The First Sunday in Advent

Lutheran	Roman Catholic	Episcopal	Common Lectionary
Jer. 33:14–16	Jer. 33:14–16	Zech. 14:4–9	Jer. 33:14–16
1 Thess. 3:9–13	1 Thess. 3:12—4:2	1 Thess. 3:9–13	1 Thess. 3:9–13
Luke 21:25–36 or Luke 19:28–40	Luke 21:25–28, 34–36	Luke 21:25–31	Luke 21:25–36

FIRST LESSON: JEREMIAH 33:14–16

The message that Israel would be justly punished by God through the instrument of foreign nations is a familiar one in the preexilic prophets. This message reached its culmination in the prophet Jeremiah, for in the Babylonian onslaughts of 597 and 587 B.C., during which time the prophet was active, all the prior words of the prophets were seen to be fulfilled (2 Kings 24:2). Jeremiah is the prophet who experiences firsthand the effects of the word of judgment he and others before him have spoken. It is therefore no coincidence that his prophetic book contains a rather extensive probe of the prophet's own interior world (see 11:18—12:6; 15:10–21; 17:14–18; 18:18–23; 20:7–13, 14–18—the Laments of Jeremiah). Such was the consequence of speaking a difficult word whose judgment provided no rider for personal exemption. The advent of God in Jeremiah's day involved breaking down and overthrowing (1:10) as the prerequisites for new building and planting.

At the level of strict historical occurrence, the Babylonian punishment did not take place in one fell swoop. The prophet sensed early in his long ministry the severity of its advent and the divine intention behind it (chaps. 2–6). As the situation worsened within Judah, the disarray was reflected most profoundly in the institution of the monarchy (chaps. 21–24), that agency established by God to ensure just rule among his people. As Babylonian pressure within the region increased, King Jehoiakim died mysteriously and was replaced by his son Jehoiachin; the eighteen-year-old Jehoiachin was then swiftly deported with leading citizenry from the capital; he was in turn replaced by his Uncle Mattaniah—a move unprecedented in the long history of the monarchy, the result of Babylonian intervention in what turned out to be the monarchy's final days. King Nebuchadnezzar gave this last king the throne name Zedekiah, "Yahweh is my righteousness" (2 Kings 24:17).

Ezekiel, the other prophet of this period, consistently questioned the legitimacy of Zedekiah, and the continuation of life in Judah beyond the events of 597 B.C. Jeremiah's own evaluation of Zedekiah appears inconsistent, due to historical or editorial factors not fully within our grasp. In the final form of the text, however, there is a cycle of oracles (chap. 22 + 21) against Judah's last four monarchs which culminates in a pronouncement of woe on "the shepherds who destroy and scatter the sheep" (23:1–2). This final word then issues into a promise of restoration, careful shepherds (23:3–4), and a Davidic scion who will be called "Yahweh is our righteousness," clearly a play on the name Zedekiah (23:5–6). In fact, the play is so close that some readers have argued the oracle was originally addressed to Mattaniah/Zedekiah, as a divine endorsement from Jeremiah at a time when his legitimacy was in question. Its present location and future reference militate against such a reading in the present canonical structure.

Our Advent passage (Jer. 33:14–16) forms a very close parallel to the text under discussion (23:5–6). Shared elements consist of common time frame ("days are coming"), common tone (security and salvation), common agent (a righteous or legitimate branch of David). Distinctive to our oracle is the application of the name "Yahweh is our righteousness" not to the Davidic shoot, but to Jerusalem (33:16). This is consistent with the new context in which the oracle appears. Jeremiah 33 focuses on the totality of restoration in all its aspects, involving the land (Judah and Israel), the city of God's special favor (Jerusalem), the cult (vv. 18–22), and the king ("righteous branch," "my servant"). The original promise (Hebrew: "the good word" of v. 14) to Israel and Judah proves far more durable than any might have expected. It outlasts both Israel's power to destroy it and the strongest blast of God's own righteous judgment in enforcing its real intention. What appeared to eyewitnesses as the final demolition (see the Book of Lamentations) proved to be the tearing down crucial for new building and planting, a return and restoration according to original intention, embracing king, cult, land, and city. With a righteous scion in place, the city could once again function within God's plan, could be in the first instance "Yahweh is our righteousness" or simply, in the language of Ezekiel, "Yahweh is there" (Ezek. 48:35).

While vividly depicting the advent of God's judgment over Judah and Jerusalem, the Book of Jeremiah also strains to see a new day and the proper establishment of God's rule, in all its fullness and intended purpose. Such an advent would emerge not simply as the longed-for reversal of present circumstances. It would occur because of them, when they were acknowledged as the tearing down and overthrowing necessary before restoration could begin. The Advent season looks at the message of hope and promise in Jeremiah within this broader framework. It recalls the original promise of God to Israel and Judah which, because divinely given, could not be demolished by the worst of human assaults. Such a promise, we learn, will stand fast in a new arena of challenge and tribulation, including even the destruction of the temple. not by Babylonian but by Roman forces, spoken of by Jesus in today's lection from Luke. But the name "Yahweh is our righteousness" will not be destroyed with the city and the temple; it forms the end-time proclamation of the returning Christ and the hope of those who suffer in his name and for the sake of God's kingdom until the second advent.

SECOND LESSON: 1 THESSALONIANS 3:9–13

At first glance, the tone and circumstance reflected in the second lesson seem altogether different from what we have observed in the Book of Jeremiah. After some delay, Paul brings to a close the prayer with which he opened the letter (1:2–10). Several distinct forms alternate in these opening chapters, but the tone of prayerful thanksgiving, such as we see it in 3:9–13, sounds a major note within Paul's address. Paul is thankful, if not surprised and proud, to learn from Timothy's report (3:6) that the fledgling church at Thessalonica has maintained its faith and love. The letter opens with this as Paul's first agenda: "We give thanks to God . . . remembering your work of faith and labor of love and steadfastness of hope in our Lord Jesus Christ" (1:2–3). In this, the earliest of Paul's letters, the apostle acknowledges the power of a message and the faith of believers, both of which are wondrously able to thrive even though he must be absent from them.

Acts 17 reports how, after only three weeks among the assembly, Paul was forced to flee by night to Beroea, and then subsequently to Athens. He must, therefore, hear of the progress (or regress) of the Thessalonians by report. The tone of thanksgiving, then, is in part accounted for by the sheer joy of witnessing growth after planting— even while absent.

But there are two other important dimensions to this letter. One is linked to the motif of thanksgiving; the other involves the phrase "at the coming of our Lord Jesus Christ with all his saints," the closing line of this Advent pericope. Paul's thanksgiving is all the more focused because he recognizes a profound dimension of faith, both in his own experience and in the faith of the Thessalonians. Leaving the predictability of idol worship "to serve a living and true God" (1:9) comes with a high cost. The rewards for such faith involve the risk of complete reorientation in resurrection faith (1:10), as well as tribulation and affliction from the external world. Paul knows this experience of faith well, and he refers to it at several points in his remarks to the Thessalonians (2:1; 3:4). He can give special thanks because the Thessalonians received the word under the conditions of affliction (1:6), even when yet greater suffering was to form part of the reward for faith (3:4). In fact, the Thessalonians have shown themselves to be "imitators of the churches of God in Christ Jesus in Judea" (2:14), and fellow sufferers with the apostle himself (3:4). Here is the source of much of Paul's joy.

One senses in the letter a naive spirit of faith and conviction, able to endure much, worthy of special treatment and sacrificial attention (2:7–8). But there is also a tone of concern in Paul's remarks that suggests such faith might be worn down by the promise of yet further trials ahead (3:5). Here we touch upon the second important dimension of the letter, which involves convictions about the Parousia. Paul mentions the second advent of Christ at several points (1:10; 2:19; 3:13; 4:13–18). Though we see nothing (and expect nothing) of a full-blown doctrine here, the positioning of these references as summarizing statements in the letter indicates the force of hopes about Jesus' imminent return within the daily struggles of the believer. The hope for a second coming, an essential element in early Christian convictions, based upon the memory of Jesus' own statements, was not the abstract fulfillment of grand designs of the Godhead. Such a return had one primary function of enabling faith to grow amidst trial and adversity. The Thessalonians could endure the affliction Paul described as "our lot" (3:3) if the wait for the Son from heaven (1:10) was an essential element in resurrection faith and a promise capable of realization in their present experience.

It is within this context that concern over "those who are asleep" (4:13) is raised; Paul's rather specific response (vv. 15–18) is directed to the broader issue of the second coming and its place within the faith and hope of the believer. Suffering and affliction are difficulties with which faith must struggle. For the Thessalonians, they are not signs of God's wrath (cf. 1:10; 2:16), but indications that the seed had been planted properly (1:6). For this community, the promise of a second advent is no ruse, but it will not eliminate hardships faith itself may create. Paul illustrates graphically the nature of the Parousia in such a way that the focus falls not on abstract timetables nor cosmic descriptions, but on resurrection hope (4:15–16) and the steady presence of the Lord (4:17). Thus Paul attempts to "supply what is lacking in their faith" (3:10), in the language of our pericope. As surely as God will direct Paul's way to the Thessalonians (3:11), though he is now absent from them, so too in times of hardship, and death itself, the presence of the Lord is directed by God to the believer. This kind of Advent hope cannot be restricted by the premature death of believers, nor by calculations and cosmic descriptions on the human plane.

GOSPEL: LUKE 21:25–36

Much critical discussion has taken place regarding this passage and its counterparts in Matthew and Mark. Questions turn on (1) the relationship between Luke's account and especially the Markan version (see Mark 13:3–37); (2) the possibility that an apocalyptic "handbill" was in circulation linking the destruction of Jerusalem with the end of the ages, available to Mark in rather pristine form and secondarily, via Mark, to Luke; and finally, (3) the precise range of the term "apocalyptic," its sociological and theological provenance, and the extent to which it involves historical timetables and especially the "last things." Comparison of Luke and Mark has suggested to some that Mark linked tightly the end of the ages and the Parousia with the destruction of the temple in Jerusalem; Luke then adjusted this scenario, from a later temporal perspective after the events of A.D. 70, to allow for an indeterminate though powerful second coming of Christ. The theory, while certainly intriguing, tends to move within its own orbit. It is also not clear that the linkage between the destruction of the temple in Jerusalem and the Parousia is all that rigid in Mark, so the adjustment motivation within Luke needs to be differently conceived. This can be shown by a brief look at Mark 13.

In Mark, as in Luke, the "apocalyptic scenario" emerges in the context of observations about the seeming permanence of the Jerusalem temple (Mark 13:1). Jesus says all this greatness will come to an end (13:2). This gives rise to the pertinent question: When will this take place and what sign will give indication that "all these things are to be accomplished" (v. 4)? A fixed sequence of expectation appears to lie behind the disciples' question. The destruction of the temple means the end of the ages; the sign is the arrival of the Son of man.

That all three parts of this linkage are in place is revealed by Jesus' lengthy response. In vv. 5–6 he says there will be many claiming to be the sign, the Son of man, or his agent. There will also be wars and tumults, but these do not mean the end (v. 7). Moreover, the desolation of the temple (the "desolating sacrilege" of Dan. 9:27) will be a significant tribulation (v. 19), without proper analogy for its significance, but even this is not the end (v. 24). The apocalyptic "end" of the ages involves a series of events. The linkage assumed by the disciples remains, but it is handled differently by Jesus, who stretches the linkage temporally. There are beginning events (v. 8), middle events (vv. 9–13, 14–23), and end events in the now wider apocalyptic age. Only then, "after that tribulation" (v. 24), will they see the Son of man coming in clouds (an explicit reference to Dan. 7:13–14).

Luke accepts this picture in general terms, and stretches the time frame even further. And there are other unique Lukan touches. Luke has spoken of the "days of the Son of man" (17:26), which suggests the possibility of proleptic occurrences of the final coming of the Son of man. So too, the nearness of the kingdom of God referred to at 21:31, and its coming without fixed signs, has its counterpart in 17:21: "Nor will they say, 'Lo, here it is!' or 'There!' for behold the kingdom of God is in the midst of you." The same language is also used concerning the "Son of man in his day" at Luke 17:23–24, which comes as suddenly but also as publicly as flashes of lightning which can fill a whole sky at once. There is also a definite resonance between the natural disturbances of 21:25, drawn with reference to the Old Testament, and the moment of death for Jesus in the crucifixion scene (Luke 23:44–45). In this regard, it is important to remember that "the Son of man coming in a cloud with power and great glory" need not refer exclusively to Jesus' coming as an end-time return to earth. In Daniel, the Son of man comes to the Ancient of Days (7:13) where he receives dominion and glory—a perspective that functions without clear reference to the end of the ages or any other fixed point in time. What Daniel sees he sees in a vision, confusing to him because relevant to a time of future tribulation.

Note how this nuance is picked up in Luke's handling of apocalyptic. At a later moment, in the second half of the Lukan drama, we see an enactment of the kind of tribulation of faith spoken of in Luke 21:12–15. In Acts 7:54–55, after a long speech inspired by the Holy Spirit (see Luke 21:15), and just before his death by stoning, Stephen "gazed into heaven and saw the glory of God . . . and the Son of man standing at the right hand of God." All this suggests that the end of the ages and the final apocalyptic consummation may confront the believer in a proleptic sense. One cannot help but think of Stephen when Jesus remarks: "When all these things begin to take place, look up and raise your heads, because your redemption is drawing near" (Luke 21:28). The final age and the coming of the Son of man are manifested on this occasion for the faithful Stephen.

At the place where we pick up the story in Luke's narrative, Jesus has already told his disciples he must go away. Something was clearly reaching its culmination in the life and death—and for a later audience, the resurrection—of Jesus. The powers of heaven were being shaken. Some elements in familiar descriptions of the end-time events, however, were not caught up in the life, death, or resurrection of Jesus. These remained dangling and confusing. Chief among these were images and concepts related to the final advent of the Son of man, a notion of "advent" ironically necessitated by the seeming lack of finality in the first advent. Since Jesus had gone away, first in death and then in ascension, in what sense had the kingdom been established, and in what sense were apocalyptic or eschatological stage props from the Old Testament still unused or unfulfilled? A different form of this same question and the dilemma it represents is to be detected in 1 Thessalonians.

Luke's response suggests that there were many potential signs of the end-time available: the appearance of messianic voices, natural disturbances, personal tribulation and persecution, and, most specifically, the destruction of the temple in Jerusalem. Luke does not deny the significance of these various occurrences, but they are all to be viewed as plain historical indications that the present age now participates in the final age. As such, the believer—in that and in every generation (see Luke 21:32)—must be ever vigilant and ready to stand before the Son of man, and not be caught as in a snare of dissipation. Individual signs are not to be decoded for what they may individually reveal about temporal calculations. They are summary indications of the sureness of the advent of the Son of man, which the believer may experience before the final day of history, in times of tribulation and testimony (Luke 21:13). Indeed, this is the time of the church.

The Second Sunday in Advent

Lutheran	Roman Catholic	Episcopal	Common Lectionary
Mal. 3:1–4	Bar. 5:1–9	Bar. 5:1–9	Bar. 5:1–9 or Mal. 3:1–4
Phil. 1:3–11	Phil. 1:4–6, 8–11	Phil. 1:1–11	Phil. 1:3–11
Luke 3:1–6	Luke 3:1–6	Luke 3:1–6	Luke 3:1–6

FIRST LESSON: MALACHI 3:1–4

It is often said that the reference to "my messenger" (Hebrew, *mal'ākî*) in our passage (3:1) gave rise to the ascription of this book to the prophet Malachi (1:1). The assumption is that this final book of the prophetic corpus, called simply "an oracle" (1:1), was originally anonymous, as were the preceding sections of Zechariah (chaps. 9–11; 12–14), also called "an oracle" (Hebrew, *massā'*). "Malachi" is said to be an unlikely form in Hebrew for a personal name, and so is more properly regarded as an appellation, "my messenger," appropriate as a title for an anonymous book, as in 1:1: "An oracle. The word of the Lord to Israel by my messenger" (or, "his messenger"). Forms like Malachi, however, are not unknown within the Old Testament (cf. Uri, Palti, Abi) and our name is likely a shortened form of Malchiyah: God is (my) messenger, or messenger/angel of God.

The coincidence of the prophet's name and the term messenger at 3:1 (see also 2:7) is explained by the increased use of this expression as a term of office in the postexilic period. Haggai is called the Lord's messenger (Hag. 1:13) and Chronicles uses the term for prophets in general (2 Chron. 36:15–16). Ecclesiastes has a passing reference to a "messenger" in a cultic setting (5:6), so the term might be a general one: "representative" of God, including Levites, priests, and prophets. This is consistent with its usage within the Book of Malachi, for in 2:7 the priest is reminded that he is "the messenger of the Lord" and in our passage the role of the messenger could be either prophetic or priestly. The final section (4:5–6) of the book as we have it seems to interpret the messenger of our passage as Elijah, the first great prophet within the prophetic canon, and one who never died but was taken bodily up into heaven (2 Kings 2:11). The one who came first will come again—at the last moment before the "great and terrible day of the Lord comes" (Mal. 4:5).

A more serious objection—related as well to the broader New Testament context in which the passage reappears—concerns the effect of identifying the messenger of 3:1 with an unknown prophet of the postexilic period. This would mean that the powerful scene of judging and cleansing spoken of in our pericope, a scene that was to precede the swiftly (3:1, 5) following advent of the day of the Lord (3:5), had already taken place in the office and lifetime of the anonymous "my messenger." This flies in the face of the energy and heightened expectation of our passage, and its broader literary context. Such an interpretation also obviously contradicts the exegesis represented by the last verses, where the coming of the messenger lies in the future and involves a figure now identified as the prophet Elijah—not "Malachi." Such exegesis could be viewed as purely speculative or corrective of the original sense, rather than integrative. But there is good reason to think such exegesis caught the essential direction of the original chapters, and our pericope specifically.

Our passage is the direct answer to the question posed in 2:17, "Where is the God of justice *(mishpāt)*?" The cynicism and dissipation reflected in such a question (recall Luke 21:34) is sharply addressed in 3:1–4 and in the following unit (3:5), which describes the nature of God's judgment *(mishpāt),* sure to come quickly. The coming of the messenger is to be an event immediately preceding the advent or theophany of God. The God they have been seeking, with ironic questions, will arrive. Before this happens, there will be a cleansing of the priests "till they present right offerings." Proper service of God having been reestablished, as in former years, God will then "come to his temple."

The sense of urgency and anticipation in our passage is not drained off by the debates that follow in the Book of Malachi—if anything, the force of God's advent is made more extreme. The final section of the book (4:4–6) most likely comes from a later hand, at a point some distance away from the perspective of our pericope. But the proclamation of the advent of the messenger, now depicted as Elijah, continues as a vital statement of hope within the community of faith. His role remains preparatory, though now not directed primarily to the "sons of Levi," but to relationships affecting full generations. It is in this same sense that Luke understands the mission of John, both in the birth narratives (see 1:17) and in the Gospel for the day (3:6).

The Baruch reading (5:1–9) sounds like a developed parallel to the poetry of Deutero- and Trito-Isaiah (Isaiah 40—55; 56—66), sections of the canonical Isaiah that were composed toward the end of the Babylonian exile and during the period of restoration (530–450 B.C.). There are many familiar themes here: *(a)* the investiture of daughter Jerusalem (Isa. 52:1) in robes not of affliction but of beauty; *(b)* the new name for Zion (Isa. 60:14; 62:4); *(c)* the return of exiles from compass points east and west (Isa. 43:5–7; 49:12); *(d)* the making of a level way (Isa. 40:3–4; 42:16); *(e)* the cooperation of the natural order (Isa. 41:17–20).

One finds in the biblical record from this period much material concerning the hopes for and the actual return of Babylonian exiles to Judah (Ezra-Nehemiah, Haggai, Zechariah). Baruch was composed in the century and a half prior to the Christian era, and so stands at some distance from Second Isaiah, the Babylonian exile, and the restoration of people, temple, and cult in the 500s. But the energy and power of the original language associated with these events has retained all its force, as the promises of God are remembered (Bar. 5:7) and viewed as still binding. Our Baruch reading continues the theme of the properly restored Zion, a theme imbedded in the Babylonian period (recall last week's Jeremiah text), but still awaiting fulfillment at the time of the composition of Baruch.

SECOND LESSON: PHILIPPIANS 1:3–11

As the Malachi text looks ahead to the advent of God, expressed in the familiar prophetic language of "the Day of the Lord," this lesson maintains the theme developed last week: thankfulness in that specific time period preceding the second advent, the day of Jesus Christ (see Phil. 1:6, 10). Here again, the unique perspective of the Advent season is reinforced by the lectionary selections. We stand between the advents, participating in the energy and movement toward the first as a way to prepare for the second, which still awaits its day. Just as the force of Mal. 3:1–4 did not lose its edge in succeeding generations, but gathered new momentum and intensity expressed in the final verses (4:5–6), so too the language of the second advent retains its power, bringing to mind the promise of Christ Jesus and the hope of the church at the earliest moment. As Paul puts it, the one who began the good work in the Philippians is the same one whose day the community awaits (1:6). With that end-time firmly in view, Jesus will bring to completion *(epiteleō)* what God had already begun among them.

As in the Thessalonian correspondence, so too here the emphasis falls upon Paul's thankfulness and heartfelt affection (1:7). Paul's sentiment is based upon factors already ("from the first day until now," v. 4) in place: the Philippians' partnership *(koinōnia)* in the gospel (v. 5) and, through grace, in Paul's imprisonment (v. 7). A sense of common cause and graceful fellowship enables Paul to experience imprisonment and hardship, and not fall prey to discouragement and dissipation—the chief enemies of the gospel and the faith of believers until the day of Jesus Christ. Again, in no small measure Paul's convictions about the coming day of Christ help shape the hope of the individual believer and the wider proclamation of the gospel. If the general critical judgment is sound, and Philippians reflects the situation of Paul's imprisonment at a fairly late point in his ministry (see Acts 24:26–28; 28:30), it is striking that appeal to "the day of Jesus Christ" has not diminished (recall Paul's use of the second advent theme in his earliest letter, 1 Thessalonians). It continues to be an integral part of the message Paul proclaims, if not the first, prayerful word from which others now follow.

In the interim, awaiting the day of Christ, Paul's prayer is that the Philippians' love will "abound more and more" with knowledge *(epignōsei)* and all discernment *(aisthēsei)*. This knowledge (consciousness) and discernment find their deepest structure not in the believer's consciousness, but in the love that Paul commends, already existing among them, ultimately rooted in the Gospel itself. Equipped with such knowledge and discernment, the community can "approve what is excellent" and be fit for the coming day of Christ (1:10).

GOSPEL: LUKE 3:1–6

It is Malachi and, more indirectly, Second Isaiah to whom we owe the notion that the "Day of the Lord" would be preceded by the coming of a messenger. The scenario is clear in Malachi, and is further developed with the interest in Elijah's return. It is less clear in Second Isaiah, where the unknown voice who cries out "prepare the way of the Lord" (Isa. 40:3) has been secondarily interpreted along the lines of Malachi's messenger. Hence the explicit juxtaposition of verses from Malachi and Isaiah in the Gospel of Mark (1:2–3). Luke cites the Isaiah passage in reference to John, son of Zechariah, and provides a fuller text (Isa. 40:3–5) than either Mark or Matthew (Matt. 3:3), probably to emphasize the mission of John and the message of God's salvation "to all flesh" (Luke 3:6; Isa. 40:5). The phrase from Isaiah "in the wilderness" (40:3) is taken to be the place of the crying voice—not the place of preparation, as in the Masoretic tradition (compare the Septuagint). The anonymous voice of Isaiah

40—often thought to be a member of the heavenly court—is now a voice with geographical identity: the wilderness. One can begin to see the coalescing with Elijah traditions even here, for Elijah had his own special days in the wilderness (see 1 Kings 19:4–18).

But in Malachi, the messenger was to prepare "the Day of the Lord," not the coming of the Messiah—a line of thought not developed in Malachi. Now, in Luke's infancy narrative (chaps. 1–2), where John is first introduced, the angelic messenger announces to Zechariah that the child to be born will fulfill the function of messenger as sketched out in Malachi: "In the spirit and power of Elijah, to turn the hearts of the fathers to the children" (1:17; Mal. 4:17). The messenger will "make ready for the Lord a people prepared" (1:17; Mal. 3:3). This Lord is the one Lord of Israel.

Now, however, with the closely following material regarding the birth of Jesus (1:26–35), called Son of God (1:32, 35), a new shift in interpretation is set up. Now, when Zechariah prophesies in the Benedictus (1:67–79) that the "prophet of the Most High" (John) "will go before the Lord to prepare his ways" (1:76), the implication is that the Incarnation is the Day of the Lord traditionally spoken of in the Old Testament. Luke 1 ends with John in the wilderness "till the day of his manifestation" (his advent as messenger) to Israel (1:80). This is where we find John in the Gospel lesson for the day.

John is introduced to us and to Israel in the precise form of literary introductions to the prophetic books (Luke 1:1–2; cf. Jer. 1:1–3). In temporally locating John during the reigns of various kings, governors, and tetrarchs, Luke imitates similar superscription data from the prophetic books, and at the same time introduces us to figures who will play a role at later points in the story. So, Annas and Caiaphas are also included, even though mention of the high priest(s) never occurs in prophetic superscriptions. The Greek of 3:2, "the word of God came to" *(egeneto rēma theou epi)* forms a close parallel (so Septuagint) to the Hebrew *(debar YHWH 'āsher hāyāh 'el)*. In preaching a baptism of repentance for the forgiveness of sins, John goes beyond the activities of the Qumran covenanters. He acts as the messenger was to act: he prepares the way of the Lord by preparing God's people. Emphasis remains here on the fulfillment of God's intentions, as spoken of by Isaiah, now on the verge of fulfillment: "And all flesh shall see the salvation of God" (Luke 3:6).

The exact identity of John is later taken up in Luke (7:18–30) because it involves the identity of Jesus and questions about the Day of the Lord. If Jesus is "the one to come," as John's disciples put it (7:19), then is he the messenger announcing the Day of the Lord? By identifying John as the "one who is to come" and the messenger of Malachi (7:27), Jesus is free to represent the Day of the Lord, and can in fact be called Lord (*kyrios,* so 7:19). Jesus is Lord and John the messenger. Jesus' life and advent is not penultimate, but ultimate.

This is not said in Luke as a diminution of John, but as a clarification of his role vis-à-vis Jesus. He remains the greatest prophet ever (7:28), Elijah first and Elijah last. And his message must be heard before one can stand before the Lord in his day. Malachi takes with utter seriousness the power of the Day of the Lord and as such recognizes the need for a time and a person of preparation lest the land be smitten with a curse (Mal. 4:6). The message of John involves a baptism of repentance, a turning, and a change of mind and heart. This is the prophetic word par excellence. It must be spoken and heard before the Day of the Lord. It is fitting that as the Age of the Prophets draws to a close, it does so in the figure of John, prophet par excellence. Only this message can prepare one for the baptism of the Holy Spirit and the irruption of the kingdom of God (7:28).

The Third Sunday in Advent

Lutheran	Roman Catholic	Episcopal	Common Lectionary
Zeph. 3:14–18a	Zeph. 3:14–18	Zeph. 3:14–20	Zeph. 3:14–20
Phil. 4:4–7 (8–9)	Phil. 4:4–7	Phil. 4:4–7 (8–9)	Phil. 4:4–9
Luke 3:7–18	Luke 3:10–18	Luke 3:7–18	Luke 3:7–18

FIRST LESSON: ZEPHANIAH 3:14–20

The Book of Zephaniah originated in the later years of the seventh century, just prior to the activity of the better known Jeremiah, during the kingship of Josiah. This is a period of waning Assyrian strength and mounting Babylonian and Egyptian influence. The "foe from the north," familiar from earlier prophetic writings, does not disappear, but is simply replaced (see Hab. 1:5–11). There is little sense of relaxation and calm in Zephaniah. The book breathes the spirit of coming judgment: "The great day of the Lord is near, near and hastening fast" (1:14). This theme of the rapidly approaching "day of Yahweh" appears frequently (1:7–9; 1:14–16; 2:2; 3:8; 3:11). The day falls upon many nations, and especially upon the Assyrians, in the manner spoken of by contemporary Nahum (Zeph. 2:13–15; Nah. 3:1–19), primarily because of their arrogance in overstepping the role given them by Yahweh (see Isa. 10:12–19).

The terror of the day, described best by Amos (5:18–20), is all the more frightening because it is unexpected. Zephaniah sees the day as one Israel can wait for (3:8), presumably because it is so near. While the day is a day of judgment for the nations (3:8), the whole earth will experience its effects. Though much of the language of Advent exults in the glorious restoration of Zion, here we stand on the far side of that restoration. The nations shall undergo a profound change, that they too might call on the name of the Lord (3:9). So too, Israel will "seek refuge in the name of the Lord" on that day (3:12), that is, after the proud and haughty are removed (3:11). The remnant on the Holy Mountain will comprise the afflicted and the poor.

There are two distinct concepts of remnant in the prophetic writings. One concept, seen for example in Jeremiah as a reflex of exodus traditions, involves the gathering and return of the dispersed, in a second exodus, from Babylon and other nations of exile. The exiles are those who, having experienced the "day of the Lord" in military defeat and deportation, now stand in a position to exult in God's promises of restoration. This is the predominant remnant theology in the Old Testament.

There is another, complementary notion of remnant. This remnant theology focuses on the "survivors" of a righteous judgment, those literally "left over" in the aftermath of military punishment. This remnant notion can be spotted in Micah, Isaiah, and Zephaniah, and it appears to be a reflex of Zion theology. In Zephaniah it involves the "humble of the land" who may be "hidden on the day of wrath of the Lord" (2:3). This same theme appears in the passage immediately preceding our Advent text: "For I will leave [lit. "make a remnant"] in the midst of you a people afflicted *['ānî]* and poor *[dāl]*" (3:12). From this remnant, a purified assembly, God can begin again.

It is in this context that daughter Zion is exhorted to sing aloud and "rejoice with all her heart" (3:14). The judgments against her have been taken away, along with her enemies (v. 15). God is in her midst (3:14, 17) not for woe but for weal, the cleansing having taken place. The "day of the wrath of the Lord" (1:3) has given way to "that day" (3:16) in which Zion is urged to "fear not" and to "that time" (3:19, 20) which has become a time of celebration. Both notions of remnant converge at the end of the pericope (vv. 19–20) as the image shifts to scenes of homecoming and return. Now the single expression "restore your fortunes" (lit. "reverse your captivity") applies in the broad sense to all those outcast in God's prior judgment, whose shame will be turned into praise (3:19).

Again, the prophetic voice testifies to the necessity of a day of powerful, cleansing judgment. Beyond this day, and within the measure of its force, a remnant will emerge capable of bearing the promises of God in exultation and rejoicing. Gathered from within and without, God will again be in their midst. Again the "fear not" of divine encouragement will be heard. As we approach the advent of our Lord expressed in the Nativity, we do so mindful that the Day of the Lord, of which Jesus is the ultimate manifestation, calls forth repentance (Luke 3:3, 8) precisely because it seeks to give way to rejoicing and exultation divinely granted. The Day of the Lord in full compass involves our death to sin because it involves, ultimately, his death. In that sense, the incarnation of God in Christ is an event, an advent, every bit as shattering of human preoccupations and perspectives as is the crucifixion itself. It is a birth T. S. Eliot termed well: "A hard and bitter agony for us, like Death, our death."

SECOND LESSON: PHILIPPIANS 4:4–9

The transition from the Old Testament lesson to Paul's letter is again worthy of note. Zephaniah looks onto a day that can be graphically described, "that time" of rejoicing, exultation, God's presence and peace, and the full "restoring of fortunes." As the final word of the Book of Zephaniah, this is a stunning vision.

Paul's words to the Philippians breathe a similar air of finality, though the content and circumstance of his appeal are different. These are, of course, not the final words of the book. There follows a description of the gift of Epaphroditus and Paul's thankful reception of it (4:10–20) before a farewell greeting and blessing (4:21–23). But there is in the short space of these six verses the spirit of culmination. The Lord is at hand (4:5). In a series of imperatives, Paul provides for the Philippians some coherent illustration of life lived on the verge of this reality. We have heard and seen in Paul the extent to which Christ's second coming has shaped the faith and hope of believers. Here, in astonishingly compact space, Paul describes the attitude, actions, and consciousness of those who live in proximity, temporal and existential, to Christ Jesus.

There is no explicit reference to the Parousia, in formal terms, such as was provided in previous weeks. The "day of Jesus Christ" spoken of in the introduction (Phil. 1:6, 10) appears only in veiled form in the expression "The Lord is at hand" *(o kyrios eggus)*. This phrase appears in conjunction with the preceding appeal to let all *(pasin anthropois)* know of their "forbearance" *(epieikes)*: a spirit of consideration and forgiveness, because of the intruding reality of Christ's presence. The community lives "on the verge of," "close to" *(eggys)* something, or someone, and the reverse is also true. This fact changes the nature of human experience and exchange. It is for this reason that while we find no strict reference to the second coming, such as we saw last week, the passage is nevertheless to be interpreted in light of this reality.

Paul acknowledges that living in light of this reality does not eliminate anxiety (v. 6). In fact, such anxiety is assumed, and the force of Paul's remarks about it indicates the power it can wield. Anxiety, worry, brooding may be constant companions for the human being who must live in the world, make decisions, seek direction and purpose in life, love, and work. Paul, however, urges that anxiety be replaced by prayer and supplication. Rather than letting anxiety wear away at the human spirit, requests are to be made known to God in everything. The concluding sentence is linked by "and" *(kai)*: "And the peace of God will keep your hearts and minds in Christ Jesus" (v. 7). There is much in life that lies beyond our ultimate control or comprehension, but the human spirit has the potential to brood over precisely these matters, as well as ones that lie within our power to change or accept. Prayer is the means by which anxiety is to be handed over to God. In exchange, the peace of God—which passes human understanding not to frustrate but to transform—will keep guard over (note the indicative: *phrouresei*) the hearts and minds of believers. Here Paul seems to articulate a rule of faith that can live with the unsureness of the timetable for Christ's return, an unsureness that could itself be converted into anxiety. The believer accepts instead the constant reality—the Lord is at hand—and sees in it the ultimate ground of hope and daily purpose.

Mention should be made as well of the opening imperative: "Rejoice in the Lord always; again, I say rejoice." Not only is anxiety to be replaced by prayer and supplication, but such prayer is also to be carried on "in thanksgiving" *(meta eucharistias)*. Rejoicing and thanksgiving involve a degree of risk, since they work best with probable cause. Again that probable cause is linked to the nearness of the Lord. One is to make supplication with thanksgiving because of the conviction of Christ's presence and the sureness of that presence working for "what is worthy of praise" (4:8). This expression concludes the virtues catalogue of v. 8, which the believer is instructed to "think about," or "take into account" *(logizomai)*. The ethical catalogue worthy of consideration is then linked to the charge of v. 9 ("Do!") as action done in imitation of Paul as apostolic teacher and model. The final statement, "the God of peace will be with you," forms a fitting conclusion, hearkening back to v. 7.

GOSPEL: LUKE 3:7–18

In his own distinctive fashion and from the perspective of his "orderly account" (1:3), Luke has clarified who John is. The infancy narrative that opens this Gospel, and last week's pericope, are particularly helpful in this regard. Now Luke shows us what John has to say. The "Word of God" on this last prophet's lips is as forceful as one might have expected from any of his predecessors.

With the term "multitudes" (cf. Pharisees/Sadducees at Matt. 3:7), Luke envisions a broader audience that John goes "into all the region of the Jordan" to address. Still, a Jewish audience is clearly implied

by the strong denunciation of vv. 8–9; it is not ruled out in vv. 10–18.
If baptism was primarily a proselyte's entry into Judaism, or even if it
was simply a cleansing rite, there is a double irony in this scene. To be
among those who came out to be baptized assumes at least a measure
of right intention; put another way, there were presumably those who
did not come out, Jewish and otherwise. John furthermore describes
their intention as involving response to warning (v. 7). Yet for John
this weighs as though nothing in the balance. Mention of the "wrath
to come" (Zeph. 2:2, 3; 3:8) is the key phrase, for it signals more than
can be treated with a water baptism or claims to have Abraham as
father. We are standing at the Day of the Lord, in the language of the
prophets, and the axe is "even now" (v. 9) laid to the root of the trees.
With this description of the stakes in the game, it should be clear to
the Jewish among the multitudes that language familiar from another
context of understanding was being used and thus had reached its
appointed time.

The situation having been clarified in as blunt a manner as possible,
the multitudes now respond about proper "fruits that befit repentance," to pick up John's words. The question is put to John bluntly
and simply: "What then shall we do?" Again, because the context in
which John works has been clarified, a simple answer is also possible.
The end-time ethic is not radically different from what had ever been
expected: care for the poor and disadvantaged through individual
sharing; proper collection of taxes; no shaking down from a position
of privilege; and contentment with wages. The ethic remains constant. What is heightened is the delivery of the ethic itself, the one
who delivers it, and the time for which it is proposed. Hence the next
question from the people, described now (v. 15) as "in expectation
and questioning *(dialogizomai)* in their hearts": "Who is this John?"

In Luke 7 the question was: Who is Jesus? Was he the messenger
of Malachi? Here the question is: Who is John? Is he the Messiah
(v. 15)? There Jesus gave the answer; here John gives it. John's ethic is
an ethic of preparation, consistent with the image of Malachi (3:2–4;
4:5–6). In the former passage, the messenger was to be a refiner and
purifier, and the question was, "Who can stand when he appears?"
The presence of John before the multitudes seems to raise the same
question, at least initially. But then John clarifies his relationship to

another one who is coming and places himself in a position below a hired servant: he is unworthy to untie his sandals (3:16).

The Day of the Lord, heralded by John, will involve a confrontation with this mightier "one who is coming." In the language of Simeon, when humanity confronts this one, the "thoughts out of many hearts (will) be revealed" (Luke 2:35). Jesus' baptism is not merely one of greater judgment, as compared with that of John. It is one capable of greater purity and refinement. The imagery of water and fire, John and Jesus, is imbedded in the Malachi pericope from last week (Mal. 3:2–3b). John has accomplished the first (as with "fuller's soap") but Jesus will complete the action with a baptism of fire and the Holy Spirit. One recalls the purification of the remnant in the prophetic literature (Isa. 4:4–5) and the granting of new spirit (Ezek. 36:26; Isa. 32:14). It is in the spirit of just such refining power that Zion and the remnant within it sing out in Zephaniah. Of course, in the present broader Lukan context, reference to the Holy Spirit brings to mind the Pentecost experience as well as the second coming of Christ, the consummation of the "days of the Son of man." Within this broader interpretive context, Luke can even characterize John's harsh words as "the preaching of Good News" *(euēggelizomai)* to the people.

The Fourth Sunday in Advent

Lutheran	Roman Catholic	Episcopal	Common Lectionary
Mic. 5:2–4	Mic. 5:2–5a	Mic. 5:2–4	Mic. 5:2–5a
Heb. 10:5–10	Heb. 10:5–10	Heb. 10:5–10	Heb. 10:5–10
Luke 1:39–45 (46–55)	Luke 1:39–45	Luke 1:39–49 (50–56)	Luke 1:39–55

FIRST LESSON: MICAH 5:2–4

In the Advent lections of the last three Sundays, the emphasis has fallen on three matters: the Day of the Lord; preparation for the day in the figure of the messenger/John; and the second advent of Christ. Now, for the first time, we encounter directly the figure of the messiah. By "messiah" we refer to "the anointed one," generally a royal figure from the house of David, Israel's first king. The term, then, has specific application within Israel and God's governance of Israel and the cosmos. It can refer to a future figure, as well as a contemporary ruler, and the time frame is determined in large measure by the circumstances under which messianic language or a messianic oracle appears. Within Jewish and Christian usage, as seen in the New Testament, the Hebrew term "messiah" (*mashiah*, "anointed [one]") has as its Greek counterpart the word "Christ" (*christos*, "anointed [one]"). Based upon the church's confession of Jesus as God's anointed one (Christ), Son of David and Son of God, the more general "messiah" is often set forth (with capital "M") "Messiah" in reference to Jesus himself. Within Jewish circles, "Messiah" may refer to a future, eschatological messiah, yet to come. Here there is point of contact with Christian convictions about the second advent.

In view of these matters, it is striking to note that the actual term *mashiah* does not appear in our Micah text, though clearly a Davidic ruler *(môshēl)* is in view. This is not unusual. As a bald term for "Davidic ruler" the term *mashiah* rarely appears in isolation (see Ps. 2:2; Hab. 3:13), and when it does, it can refer to a one other than a royal figure (i.e., priest) or even a non-Israelite (Cyrus the Persian in Isa. 45:1). Terms other than "anointed one" appear more frequently: "branch"; "servant"; "chosen one"; "shepherd"; "shoot."

As is true of many prophetic texts that speak of a coming—imminent or future—Davidic figure (see Isa. 9:2–7; 11:1–9; Jer. 23:1–6), there is debate about the historical period in which our passage emerged. Many argue that the promise of a new Davidide presupposes the full destruction of the kingdom, such as Israel experienced in the Babylonian defeat and exiling of 597 and 587 B.C. This would make the relevant passages exilic or postexilic additions to the original prophetic tradition. Others reckon that such texts could well have emerged at any period when kingship was at low ebb (and there are several good possibilities here) and hopes were high for new and proper leadership.

There is clear evidence in Micah of secondary additions to a core eighth-century text, so the possibility that our passage is among them cannot be ruled out of court. But such a conclusion is by no means required. Micah is remembered in Jeremiah's day (see Jer. 26:18–19) as the prophet who called for the fall of Jerusalem; the text cited at Jeremiah's trial is Mic. 3:12: "Therefore because of you Zion shall be plowed as a field; Jerusalem shall become a heap of ruins." The "you" of Micah's indictment includes leadership in Zion and throughout "Jacob/Israel" (1:5; 2:12; 3:1, 9). This is a favorite expression of Micah's, reminiscent of the old Unified Kingdom of David's day. Use of the term "ruler" *(môshēl)* in our passage, together with "heads of Jacob" and "rulers of the house of Israel" (3:9) hearkens back to the early days of kingship and actual unity among the twelve tribes— from before *(miqqedem)* and "from ancient days" *(mîmê 'ôlām),* as in 5:2. It is quite possible, therefore, that in the midst of dire predictions of destruction (see 1:8–16), Micah called for a reestablishment of Davidic rule (he avoids the term "king," Hebrew, *melek*) along original guidelines. Micah speaks of a return to Bethlehem Ephrathah, the little tribe (see 1 Sam. 16:1–13 for the anointing of David), where David will be raised up again to "stand and feed his flock in the strength of the Lord" (5:4) as the good shepherd and ruler. "For now" *(kî 'attāh)*—the signal for reversal—"he shall be great to the ends of the earth" (5:4).

Somewhat confusing imagery sketches out the timetable for the birth of the ruler in 5:3. The reference to "give them up" seems to operate with God as subject. God will hand over Zion and her inhabitants, and the unknown "judge" of Israel (5:1)—a figure who stands in contrast to the coming ruler—until the mother of the new Davidide has brought forth (cf. Isa. 7:14). Then the remainder of Israel shall return to the rule of this reestablished shepherd-king.

Micah sets into motion a trajectory of hope regarding proper Davidic rule. The One to come, in his day, is like the one from of old, the original David. At points, the language sounds as though he is the original David, brought back again at a time of distress and upheaval. This messianic trajectory remains alive within a now broader scriptural context, reflecting centuries of struggle and a constant pressing for fulfillment. Within the context of New Testament faith, it is no easy claim to call Jesus God's Christ. On the one hand, Jesus seems to explode the original sense and context in which the term was to apply—though a glance at developing messianic hopes reveals the seeds of transformation already at work. On the other hand, calling Jesus "Christ" signals the goal of the trajectory in such final terms that there can now be no hiding from the claims this one makes and that the language about him, applied to him, seeks to make. The questions only shift: Where do we see his rule? And where not?

The personal and social implications of these questions are so far-reaching that a return to Bethlehem is unavoidable. We must hear again the language of prophetic hope in order to see what an awesome, scandalous thing it was to talk about "fulfillment" in this man from Nazareth—or, for that matter, in any one. It is far easier to leave the language of prophetic hope in the realm of soaring rhetoric or distant vision; it is more difficult to say such language had in fact reached its appointed goal. What, then, of our deepest visions and hopes? Are they to be summed up in this One? This question represents the challenge of Advent faith.

Having said this, it must be added that the images of hope and promise associated with prophetic vision are not drained of their vital force when one calls Jesus "Christ." Rather they are sharpened to a new intensity as the kingdom of God is brought straight into our midst. There can now be no avoiding the prophetic hope or its final goal in Jesus of Nazareth, "Christ" Jesus. Such are the demands of a kingdom brought close, not a chapter closed or a deferred hope halfheartedly recognized as valid. So too our hopes must in the end look to this man from Nazareth, with the same intensity and with every bit as much force and conviction as is represented by centuries of prophetic word and promise to Israel. In this man Jesus, God demonstrates his faithfulness to promises of old, while at the same time reaching out to those of us in later generations who now see in the concrete promises to Israel a witness and example of the concrete promises made by God in Christ Jesus for all ages.

SECOND LESSON: HEBREWS 10:5–10

It seems unusual to enter the world of Hebrews three full weeks into Advent. The focus of the second lesson in previous weeks has been on "the day of Jesus Christ" and the significant place hopes about the second advent have in the life of believers. Moreover, the message of Paul has brought us into contact with specific communities and their struggles for faith. In the second lesson for today, emphasis on the person and intention of Christ is so predominant that the professing author and the addressed community all but fade from view. This factor is not unusual to our pericope, but informs the full narrative presentation of the Book of Hebrews, raising many questions about the date, the author, and the audience for such a message, titled only "to the Hebrews." Does the book's preoccupation with the priesthood and temple cult mean it can be dated safely before A.D. 70 and the destruction of the Jerusalem temple? Or is interest in these matters determined by theme—the sacrifice of Christ—and by Hebrews' special interest in the Scriptures, whose picture of priesthood and cult is the essential starting point for discussion and modification? What kind of an author would employ such a midrashic style, closely akin to Jewish argumentation; would work with a notion of a preexistent Christ (1:2) familiar from John, but maintain an interest in matters Pauline (obedience in faith; God's promises to Abraham; new access to God); and would still feel free to develop themes completely unique to his own presentation, often termed the longest sustained argument in the New Testament? Martin Luther suggested Apollos (Acts 18:24–28), and if nailing down the author was an important key to interpretation, his guess would be as good as any. In sum, matters of date, authorship, and audience are elusive; discussion of them returns us to the text itself and its profound and unique message.

Our pericope forms one link in a long argument—it begins with the inferential *dio* ("consequently" or "for this reason")—involving a description of the characteristics and effects of Christ's sacrifice (9:11—10:18). In our passage the argument is developed on the basis of a Scripture text, Psalm 40 (Masoretic; 39 Septuagint). In both texts, the original message is fairly clear. A contrast is established between two forms of obedience, what God "desires" (Hebrew, *ḥāp-hastā;* Greek, *ēthelēsas*): ritual offerings or the sacrifice of an attentive ear, which God has prepared (Hebrew = "carved out") in mortals. The RSV offers an interpretation of this somewhat obscure image in Psalm 40: "Sacrifice and offering thou hast not desired; but thou hast given me an open ear" (v. 6). For reasons unclear, Hebrews either reads another text here or works with a more expansive image: "But a body (not *ōtia* ["ear"] but *sōma*) hast thou prepared for me." This verse is the pivot in the argument. When Christ entered the world *(kosmos),* he did so with a body prepared for sacrifice. So now the contrast is not simply between ritual—external obedience—and moral—internal obedience—as sketched in the Psalm. Rather, it is between the willful, intentional obedience of Christ who consciously sacrificed himself in suffering and death and the patently unconscious animal who is a passive victim. Thus it was concluded in 10:4: "For it is impossible that the blood of bulls and goats could take away sins."

This interpretation is stressed in the exegesis the author of Hebrews supplies in 10:8–10. The emphasis falls on "that will" *(thelēma)* of Christ. In the Hebrew, "doing the will of God" was what the psalmist said was his desire and delight (Ps. 40:8), and the verb is the same one used of God in 40:6. So too, through the sacrifice of his body, the will of Christ and the will of God were congruent, as had been written of him in "the roll of the book," that is, the Scriptures available to the author of Hebrews. The pericope ends with a description of the benefits of this action: "and by that will we have been sanctified through the offering of the body of Jesus Christ once for all" (10:10). Now we have an access to God (10:19) only foreshadowed in the cultic ritual granted by God to Israel.

Emphasis on the willful action of Christ may seem ill-fitted to this last Sunday of Advent. The Nativity to follow traditionally focuses on the infant Jesus, hardly in a position to consciously effect any such grand designs. But what was seen in the end by the author of Hebrews we affirm to have been there from the very beginning: a sacrifice of service and obedience which had its point of departure in simple bodily existence, beginning with birth and a full sharing of our mortality. Hebrews is able to do as full justice to this birth as to the death, inseparable in their significance:

> Since therefore the children share in flesh and blood, he himself partook of the same nature, that through death he might destroy him who has the power of death, that is, the devil, and deliver all those who through the fear of death were subject to lifelong bondage. (Heb. 2:14)

As we move ever closer to the manger, the full mystery and power of what it means for God to take on flesh looms before us, as well as Christ's mature sacrifice of love and obedience:

> Therefore he had to be made like his brothers and sisters in every respect, so that he might become a merciful and faithful high priest in the service of God, to make full expiation for the sins of the people. For because he himself has suffered and been tempted, he is able to help those who are tempted. (Heb. 2:17–18)

The priesthood is high because it is bestowed on one who for our sakes became so low in birth, obedience, and death.

GOSPEL: LUKE 1:39–56

The Magnificat (Luke 1:46–55) is Mary's hymn of praise to God. She utters the canticle in response to Elizabeth's own spirit-filled declaration concerning her (1:42–45). We learn two key things from Elizabeth. The promised conception (1:31) has indeed occurred (1:42), and the child to be born is not just great (1:32), holy, and even the Son of God (1:35), but *kyrios,* Lord (1:43), seemingly indistinguishable from the Lord Mary herself praises in 1:46. Elizabeth extolls Mary's faith in trusting what the angel had promised. She is "blessed" *(makaria),* in contrast to the incredulous Zechariah (1:18).

Most scholars think Luke has spliced the Magnificat into his carefully composed Infancy Narrative (chaps. 1–2). It has its own self-contained quality and is probably best understood as a Jewish Christian hymn developed independently of the Gospel, perhaps in early worship contexts. It is reminiscent of Hannah's prayer-song in 1 Sam. 2:1–10, though Hannah forms a better parallel to Elizabeth than to Mary. Other Old Testament sources can be identified in the hymn, especially from the Psalter. The Magnificat is rather loosely connected to the specific situation of Mary and Elizabeth. It does find attachment in Mary's sense of thanksgiving and beatitude (v. 48), related to her conceiving and the impending birth. But it goes beyond this individual response of praise to extoll God's attention to the poor and the lowly, and those who fear him in every generation. Israel is God's servant in just such need of help. The promises of God, stretching back to Abraham, are coming to fruition.

In the case of Elizabeth and Zechariah, the motif of barrenness was combined with old age, bringing to mind Abraham and Sarah. Mary's situation, parallel in so many ways, goes yet one step further. She is only a "virgin betrothed" (1:27) and has not as yet had relations with a man (1:34). How can the promise of the angel, concerning the birth of a king, be believed? As in Elizabeth's case, the answer is returned to Mary: with God nothing is impossible (1:37). With humans, however, much is impossible, including belief in the promises of God. But Mary "hears the word of God and keeps it," as her own son will put it at a later point in the story (11:28). For this, she is blessed.

The interplay between John and Jesus is brilliantly constructed by Luke. Even in the womb, the messenger delivers messages, in the power of the Holy Spirit, to Elizabeth, in recognition of the mother of the Lord and the Lord himself. John's leaping in the womb (v. 44) recalls the struggling of Jacob and Esau within Rebekah, the barren one whose husband Isaac's prayer was answered (the same verb of Luke 1:44, *eskirtēsen* ["leaped"], is used in Gen. 25:22, LXX). The leaping in Genesis is to be interpreted as a different kind of signal: of tension to come, a vying for first-birth with all its rights and privileges, younger and elder, stronger and weaker, service in resentment.

In Luke, however, the one to be born first acknowledges the greatness of the one six months (1:26) his junior. John is the first, who becomes the last and greatest of the prophets. Jesus is the second, who represents the first hope of all the prophets who went before John. We have entered a new age, heralded by leaping not in jealousy but in extreme joy *(agalliasei)*, the kind of joy the angel Gabriel promised would be Elizabeth's at the birth of John (1:14). In short space the promise is kept, even before the birth of her own son, in a surprise confrontation with the mother of her Lord. Within Elizabeth, in the person of John, the entire prophetic age is collapsed that it might stand just months shy of the Day of the Lord, and be stunned into joy by the nearness of its approach. For the next three months (1:56) Mary and Elizabeth stand side by side in expectation. On this note we await the Nativity not of John, whose mission has been made clear, but of Jesus, whose advent leaps among us with full force and extreme joy.

The Nativity of Our Lord, Christmas Day

Lutheran	Roman Catholic	Episcopal	Common Lectionary
Isa. 62:10–12	Isa. 52:7–10	Isa. 9:2–4, 6–7	Isa. 9:2–7
Titus 3:4–7	Heb. 1:1–6	Titus 2:11–14	Titus 2:11–14
Luke 2:1–20	John 1:1–18 or John 1:1–5, 9–14	Luke 2:1–14 (15–20)	Luke 2:1–20

FIRST LESSON: ISAIAH 62:10–12 AND ISAIAH 9:2–7

It is now commonplace to posit a distinction between chaps. 40–55 and 56–66 as Second and Third Isaiah, respectively. They are chiefly distinguished by their temporal perspective: Third Isaiah coming after the exile, in Judah, struggling with the restoration; Second Isaiah composed during the exile in Babylon.

As we see in this pericope, however, they have much language in common. Periodically, exact quotations of Second Isaiah seem to appear in chaps. 56–66. Isaiah 62:10 is reminiscent of 52:11 and especially 40:3–5, with its charge to build and prepare a way; 62:11 recalls 40:10, with its image of God's return with his reward and recompense. There seems to be a stock language that forms the building blocks of both Second and Third Isaiah's poetry: "highway" (cf. 40:3); "way" (cf. 40:3); "ensign" or "standard" (cf. 49:22); "daughter Zion" (cf. 52:2). Common language is generally explained as a disciple's imitation or further development of the master's original poetry. But this is pure speculation and the differences between Second and Third Isaiah ought not be overplayed.

Our passage, for example, cannot sustain too strict a temporal distinction between Second and Third Isaiah. The same language and tone of expectation and preparation found in the pivotal chap. 40 is still maintained here. Zion still awaits the return of the dispersed and a sign of God's presence; her imminent salvation (or Savior, LXX) is still a matter of ardent hope (v. 11). With the return of exiles and God, Zion will receive a new name ("Not Forsaken"), and the returned will be called "people of the Holy One" (RSV, "the holy people").

The opening imperative "pass, pass" (v. 10) is linked by preposition ("through"; "into") to the noun "gates," but it is not clear just what gates are meant. Are these gates of the city or of the temple (note the preceding reference to the sanctuary in v. 9)? Critics generally assume the former and develop the image of people passing through gates to go outside and build up a "way of the people," that is, a way for exiles to return. Others interpret the "way of the people," and even the "highway" from Second Isaiah in a more metaphorical, inward sense. Note that there is no reference to wilderness and desert as in chap. 40 ("In the wilderness prepare the way of the Lord, make straight in the desert a highway"). The "way of the people" (cf. "way of the Lord" and "highway of our God" in Isaiah 40) would then be their moral and religious life, which must be cleared of stones in order that they might be "the people of the Holy One" (62:12).

Both senses of the "way" (human/divine; inward/outward) are relevant to this Nativity celebration. John has been sent to prepare the way, and we have heard his message in Advent. Now we are to pass through the gates not of temple, nor of city, but of the Bethlehem stable, in order to be called "People of the Holy One." In the person of Jesus, whose name means salvation (Isa. 62:11), God himself passes through gates to "seek us out" (v. 12), that we might "not be forsaken" (v. 12), but might return "glorifying and praising God for all we have heard and seen as it had been told to us" (Luke 2:20). The preparation is completed as Advent gives way to Nativity.

The second passage for Christmas day is also from Isaiah (Isa. 9:2–7). It too speaks of reversal—from darkness to light and from sorrow and defeat to joy (9:2–3). The boots and bloody garments and battle gear are burned "as fuel for fire" (9:5). Judah has witnessed the fall of the Northern Kingdom and the overrunning of its own small territory during the Assyrian period. But the former times for Zebulon and Naphtali are about to turn into the latter days of eschatological promise (9:1).

All this will come about because of the birth of a child (9:6). There are other places in Isaiah where hopes are pinned on the imminent birth of a young child (e.g., the sign for Ahaz, Isa. 7:14). But there the child remains mysterious: we know only his name, Immanuel (God-with-us), and in some sense he is more like the other mysterious children of the prophet himself (Remnant-Returns, Swift-Booty, Hasty-Prey), whose significance lies in the force of their names more than in their actions or personalities. Is Immanuel even a king from what we can tell of 7:14–17? Also, the events associated with his birth and growth are events both of weal and woe (7:15–25).

Not so our child in Isa. 9:2–7; not one note of ambiguity here. The prophet gives way to an outpouring of joy and optimism almost without analogy in the Old Testament. In the description of the child who will be king, the images are compounded one upon another (vv. 6–7). The reversal in 9:2–5 is entirely predicated on the birth of this one. This was to be kingship in its most powerful expression, as witnessed by the titles for the child (9:6) and the quality of his reign (9:7).

How could all of these hopes and convictions rest upon the shoulders of a child—an infant whose destiny lay totally before him? Clearly more was at stake than optimistic character assessment or prognostication on the part of the prophet Isaiah. Such would be the kingship of this child because it was the expression of God's intended will for kingship: "To establish it, to uphold it, with justice and righteousness, from this time forth and forever more" (v. 7). Only the "zeal of the Lord of hosts" could do a thing so preposterous. The kingship of Jesus will give way to further penetration into the mystery of God's will for kingship and kingdom. This Christmas morning, he is inaugurated with a manger for a throne.

SECOND LESSON: TITUS 3:4–7 AND TITUS 2:11–14

There are two different sections of Titus used for the second lesson of the Nativity. They are, however, cut from the same cloth and can easily be treated together.

Titus, with 1 and 2 Timothy, is generally classified a pastoral epistle. Debates persist about actual Pauline authorship and continuity with authentic Pauline thought. Reference to specific forms of church leadership (elders and bishops, Titus 1:5–9) and matters of administration and proper conduct suggests a more advanced—the term institutional is often used—form of Christian fellowship.

Examples of formal ethical (virtue and vice) codes are found in 2:1–10 and 3:1–3, passages that frame our Christmas lectionary texts. It has been stated, quite correctly, that many of the concerns in these listings fall into a category one might reasonably expect to represent the minimum code of conduct (no pilfering; no slavery to drink or various passions; love of spouse; no hating each other). Bishops are not to be violent drunkards (1:7); elders are not to have wild and uncontrolled children (1:6). In what kind of climate must reference to these rudimentaries be explicitly made? Things are apparently at such low ebb in Crete, and the leaders and people in need of such remedial exhortation, that even a "prophet of their own" can conclude: "Cretans are always liars, evil beasts, lazy gluttons" (1:12). What an odd text and context for Christmas morning reflection!

But, of course, these instruction lists are not read in their entirety for Nativity. Rather, in both instances (2:11–14; 3:4–7), what we get is the motivation clause for the behavior and attitudes enjoined, which vary from age to age within differing social contexts. This is quite apparent in 2:11 with the consequential "for" *(gar)* and in 3:4, where a rather artificial starting point breaks up the flow in the argument beginning at 3:3. Minimum standards of social conduct and order are not held up for their own inherent commendability. They flow from the bottom-line experience of the Christian: the onslaught of God's grace *(epephanē,* see 2:11; 3:4) which came not by virtue of our righteousness, but God's mercy (3:5). This experience moves with its own formative tendency, called here "training" (or "education," *paideousa,* 2:12). Even though the Pastorals are letters composed at some distance from the historical origin of the kerygma, it is the rudimentary experience of Christian faith, received now in baptismal washing (3:5), to which appeal is made as the ground of proper conduct within the community.

At this same historical distance, neither have convictions about the second advent been spiritualized or replaced by new formulations. The first advent still calls forth the second: "Awaiting our blessed hope, the appearing of the glory of our great God and Savior Jesus Christ" (2:13). The doing of good deeds (2:14)—even the zealous exchange of gifts this season—is not the consequence of adherence to rudimentary social mores upon which any good culture is founded. Rather, such doing of good deeds springs from the formed baptismal will, which recalls with thanksgiving that first birth and which looks ahead with joy and confidence to the second advent of our Savior.

GOSPEL: LUKE 2:1–20

This is an amazing story. One might assume that familiarity and constant rereadings would dull its edge and blunt its ability to communicate to hearers the power of God's action in Bethlehem. But some new facet of the gem is always waiting to be polished so it can shine with its intended brilliance.

"Now in those days an edict *(dogma)* was issued that the whole world *(oikoumenē)* should be registered" (Luke 2:1). The sonorous tone of this opening statement was surely intended by Luke. Measured by standards of any age, a worldwide census would be an act requiring incredible human ingenuity and patience, and the marshaling of various reluctant forces within civil administration. It would be an act rivaling heavenly administration.

Luke doubtless wishes to relate the birth of Jesus to the *Pax Augusta* and relevant world history. Such is the scope of his canvas and the larger concern of his Gospel undertaking (1:1). But in the end, the grand civil engineering of Rome results in a consequence unforeseen: the movement of Joseph and Mary to Bethlehem and a subtle coordination of Jesus' birth with the ancient place of David. Luke feels no need to call attention to this fact by, for example, citing Mic. 5:2 ("But you, O Bethlehem Ephrathah") or some other relevant Old Testament text. It is part of the scheduled movement of Mary and Joseph and the divine will within the messiness of a worldwide census. But then how quickly the story moves to its heart: birth and the promises of angels to shepherds (2:6–18). The most heavenly and the most earthly is the vista against which the impressive designs of Caesar Augustus are measured. Then human achievement even of the grandest order pales considerably.

With the interest in enrollments (vv. 1, 2, 3, 5), there is ironically no registration for Mary and Joseph in a simple lodging place: "And she gave birth to her first-born son and wrapped him in swaddling cloths, and laid him in a manger, because there was no place for them in the inn" (2:7). Should our hearts go out to the infant and the family because they seem cast off at such a time? Or is this event too momentous for inn or manger or even some more suitable, perhaps impressive space? Just what kind of place would be suitable? Exclusion is not finally possible from either a divine or human perspective. Only delay and inconvenience. This thing must happen, as any father and mother know, and the where becomes incidental to the fact itself, stated here with utter simplicity: "And while they were there, the time came for her to be delivered, and she gave birth . . . " (2:6). Jesus, Lord and Christ, is born in the same way you and I come into the world.

The magnificence that does ensue involves other parties not privy to the actual birth scene. The birth has already occurred when the action shifts to shepherds "in that region" who, by dint of vocation, are outdoors and up at night. Now the significance is transmitted with all the glory of the Lord (v. 9). Here is a theophany to rival any Old Testament scene, with angels, with glory, and with fear. The theophany takes the form of a message: "Good news *(euaggelizomai)* of great joy." The Messiah, the Lord *(christos kyrios)* has been born in David's city, an identity already made known to the parents of John and Jesus, now revealed to the world at large, through the agency of these unknown shepherds. The provision of a sign for the shepherds (v. 12), reminiscent of the Old Testament world, could be no more direct: it is the child himself, in a simple manger. What is wondrous is their knowing just who this child is and their later reporting of the fact (vv. 17–18).

The scene closes with Mary "pondering all these things and keeping them in her heart." The same phrase will be used again at 2:51, after Jesus is grown and has remained in the temple, rather than return with his parents to Nazareth. There is no static and complete comprehension of what God is doing in Jesus. Faith always seeks understanding and movement to new faith. Mary can act in faith even when full understanding is lacking (1:38); she can give praise in the Magnificat (1:47) and then stand as others give similar praise (1:20).

The titles provided (Lord, Messiah) right at the beginning of the Gospel, which are meant to clarify who this child is, have been grafted from the postresurrection experience of the church (Acts 2:36). The Holy Family, the shepherds, and we the readers all know who this one is, before he is born and as he now lies as an infant in the manger. This could result in an artificial or mechanical portrayal. But the opposite turns out to be the case. From the very start, the truth of who Jesus is demands a turning over in the heart, and a deep pondering *(symballeō)*. Knowing who Jesus is, measured against the promises of God, only establishes the arena in which faith can be found and in which faith can grow, knowing its source and its hope. It is this Jesus who is the Christ of Israel, Lord of all peoples, hope of all ages. The story tells us this at the start. But now the difficult chapter begins. Now we must watch as Jesus exercises his kingship and lordship, the significance of which Mary senses and which will become increasingly clear as "he increases in wisdom and stature" (3:52). The identity of this˙ one means worship and praise, discipleship and service.

The First Sunday after Christmas

Lutheran	Roman Catholic	Episcopal	Common Lectionary
Jer. 31:10–13	Sir. 3:2–6, 12–14	Isa. 61:10—62:3	1 Sam. 2:18–20, 26 or Sir. 3:3–7, 14–17
Heb. 2:10–18	Col. 3:12–21	Gal. 3:23–25; 4:4–7	Col. 3:12–17
Luke 2:1–52	Luke 2:41–18	John 1:1–18	Luke 2:41–52

FIRST LESSON: JEREMIAH 31:10–14 AND 1 SAMUEL 2:18–20, 26

Jeremiah 30—31 is often referred to as "The Book of Consolation," a title taken from the introductory unit 30:1–3, where Jeremiah is instructed to "write in a book all the words that I have spoken to you" (30:2). The contents of this book *(sēpher)* involve the restoration of Israel. As such, they stand in some contrast to the bulk of the

Jeremiah tradition, which focuses on the punishment of Yahweh and the coming destruction of Judah. But God's "restoring the fortunes" (30:3, 18; 31:23), the promise of a new covenant (31:31), and the joyous return to Zion (30:17; 31:6, 12) are matters not entirely unanticipated in surrounding chapters. At Jeremiah's call we learned that God's plans involved building and planting as well as overthrowing and tearing down (1:10). Here, at a central point in the book, and in a more sustained fashion than we have yet witnessed (cf. 3:15–18; 23:3–8; 29:10–14), we see the nature of that rebuilding intention.

The historical question—Did Jeremiah actually speak/write these words?—involves a complicated set of factors. Literary affiliation with Second Isaiah (note the frequent address to Israel/Jacob) and even the Ezekiel traditions (31:29–30, 33, 38–40) can be detected, suggestive of an exilic date and provenance. But the influence of Hosea has also been argued (31:2–6), and the possibility exists that some of these poems originated at a period when Jeremiah longed for the restoration of the old Northern Kingdom (31:15–22) in tones reminiscent of chaps. 2–4 and his early prophetic career. The final editing of "The Book of Consolation" has sought to make clear the application of the message to both "Israel and Judah" (30:3) and "all the families of Israel" (31:1), whatever its point of historical origin. In the present shape of the material, there is an evenly distributed interest in Jacob, Israel, Judah, Ephraim, and Zion. Just as Jeremiah's words have effect across every social and geographical boundary, reaching even to Egypt (chap. 44) and Babylon (chaps. 27–29), so too his word of restoration involves "all the families of Israel." "And they shall be my people" (31:1).

Our pericope opens with an appeal to the nations and coastlands to witness the gathering by God of Israel, a familiar motif from Second Isaiah (41:1; 42:10; 49:1). Such an action requires divine force, for the punishing nations are "too strong for him" (v. 11); Israel must be ransomed *(ge'ālô)* by a yet stronger agent. With images developed in the surrounding context, gathered Israel will return to a land now rich with fertility and bounty, provided by the one Lord who rules both historical and natural realms. So surely as God made the fruitful land a desert (4:26), God would now make their life "like a watered garden" (v. 12). Joy, comfort, and gladness are exchanged for the mourning and sorrow of defeat and deportation (v. 13). The priests who bore responsibility for failing to teach Israel God's ways (2:8) are now recipients of abundance (31:14). Israel failed to "turn back" *(shûb)* to God (4:1). But God did not fail to "turn back the fortunes" *(shûb shebût)* of Israel.

The passage from 1 Sam. 2:18–20, 26 was clearly chosen as a parallel to the Gospel lesson for Christmas 1. There we read of the parents of Jesus traveling yearly to Jerusalem for Passover (Luke 2:41), on this occasion with their twelve-year-old son Jesus. Here we read of the boy Samuel ministering at the house of the Lord (1:24) at Shiloh, and of his mother's yearly visit to him (2:19). In the Gospel lesson, tension exists between the (unannounced) decision of Jesus to stay in Jerusalem and the expectation of his parents, who learn of this decision after the fact and rather bluntly. Here there is no such tension, since the child Samuel had been dedicated ("lent") to service of God by the thankful Hannah (1:27), whose prayer God had answered. The yearly travel to Shiloh had once been marked by sad reminders of Hannah's barren state (1:3–8), with weeping and distress. Now it is marked by the memory of the prayer and the vow she had once made, both of which had been fulfilled, by God and by her. Eli, aware of the vow and the commitment of Hannah to it, asks that the Lord grant her yet more children, a prayer answered with the birth of three sons and two daughters (2:21).

Samuel will continue to "grow in stature and in favor with the Lord and with men" (1 Sam. 2:26). This is, however, the last we hear of the blessed Hannah, who now fades from view (though see Luke's interest in the eighty-four-year-old prophetess Anna at 2:36–38). The Gospels maintain their interest in the figure of Mary. In this one who stands in a position of obvious closeness to Jesus, we see the paradox of seeming proximity. Her son is the Lord, the one who must be about his heavenly Father's business (Luke 2:49), whose childhood trip to Jerusalem, while troubling for confused parents, only foreshadows a more traumatic journey later and a different kind of day in the temple (Luke 19:45—21:38), where listening and questioning (2:46) give way to cleansing, teaching, trial, and death. This is the one whose family now extends to all nations, kindreds, and tongues.

SECOND LESSON: HEBREWS 2:10–18

Using the Psalms and other scriptural references, the author of Hebrews first mounts a persuasive defense of the superiority of the Son over the angels (1:5—2:9). The only direct reference to this argument in our passage is found at 2:16. But here it is not Jesus' proper relationship to the angels that is the topic of discussion, but the superiority of humanity to the angels as targets of God's sanctifying action in Christ: "For surely it is not with angels that he is concerned but with the descendants of Abraham" (2:16).

The chief burden of our passage is that Jesus was the pioneer *(archēgon)* who was made perfect *(teleiōsai)* through suffering *(dia pathēmatōn)*. The verb related to perfection occurs frequently in Hebrews and has to do with Jesus' qualifications to serve as pioneer and high priest *(archiereus)*. He is deemed worthy or perfect to cleanse and sanctify.

In a manner of argumentation familiar from our Advent 4 pericope (Heb. 10:5–10), the author of Hebrews mounts a case with the aid of Old Testament texts, here drawn from Psalms (Masoretic, 22:23; LXX, 21:23) and Isaiah (8:16–17). There is only very slight divergence from the LXX tradition in these citations, in contrast to what we saw in chap. 10. Jesus is depicted as the speaker of these texts, taking up the anonymous first-person speech of the Psalmist and the voice of the prophet Isaiah (see also 2 Sam. 22:3) in order to stress his brotherhood with humanity. He proclaims God's name to his brothers *(adelphois mou)* and is perfected because he puts his trust in God (v. 13), in the language of Isa. 8:16. The children God has given him (v. 13) are not the sign-children of Isaiah (see Isaiah 7—8), but all humanity, the children with whom he shares flesh and blood (v. 14) and with whom he shares a common origin (v. 11).

Jesus is a "pioneer" in the true sense of the word because he alone blazes a trail ahead of us, defeating death by enduring suffering and incapacitating the one who gives death its paralyzing tyranny over us. This cannot be done at a distance. Life and death must be shared in the fullest terms. There is no partial living any more than there is partial dying. In facing death, Jesus too had to endure the temptation, familiar to all of us, to do other than trust in God. As a result he can on the one hand know our temptations as we know them but is also worthy to stand as faithful high priest and cleanse us from sins we commit when we do not trust in God. This is his chief service to God and humanity (v. 18).

To hear this text in the Christmas season is to be reminded of the full humanity of Jesus, how his birth in Bethlehem was a birth precisely like our own. Jesus saves us and grants us full access to God, even though we are bound by our sins and therefore separated from God, by becoming like us in every respect, but also unlike us in one key respect: as the sole one among us who goes before us as pioneer to willingly suffer and conquer death. By this action he is perfected and made equal to his task as *archēgon*. Even in the manger, Jesus begins his pioneering effort on our behalf. As a child, he must be about the business of his Father, a business that has to do with our salvation and his victory over death. The joy of Christmas has to do with this victory, and with Christ's full sharing of himself with us, taking on our nature, our life and our death, in order to grant us new life in his name.

This theme of eucharistic fellowship finds expression in the other lectionary choice for the second lesson, from Colossians 3:12–17. As in last week's lesson from Titus, our text is sandwiched between the largely negative admonitions of 3:5–11 and the following household code of 3:18—4:1. Our pericope is again the motive-clause for what precedes and follows. The link with the foregoing is established with the conjunction "therefore" (*oun*—RSV, "then") of 3:12. The triad "chosen, holy, beloved" is a Pauline favorite, derived from similar usage in the Old Testament as a description of Israel, now transferred to the New Israel, those forgiven and in fellowship with the Lord Christ. With its tone of thanksgiving and expansive exhortation ("whatever you do in word or deed, do everything in the name of the Lord Jesus"), it is a fitting passage for this First Sunday after Christmas. After the long Advent preparation, it is now time to "sing psalms and hymns and spiritual songs with thankfulness" in our hearts to God (3:16).

GOSPEL: LUKE 2:41–52

There are several matters of psychological interest—and confusion—in this brief episode in Jerusalem that beg the reader's attention. One has to wonder how Mary and Joseph failed to notice Jesus missing for a whole day. Were there special traveling arrangements? Did specific groups journey separately? What was Jesus doing for this whole three-day (v. 46) period? Where did he spend the night? Or, more pointedly, how could Jesus have such fundamental disregard for his parents and keep them in the dark about his intentions?

Luke does not feel compelled to supply the details that would make a good human interest story, but seems content with the terse explanations he does offer ("his parents did not know"; "but supposing him to be . . . "). The narrative adopts its own set of priorities, with specific matters of psychology and historicity set to the side. One notices that the movement of the narrative in the opening verses (41–46) is especially compact. The reader is propelled through an extended series of events—Passover trip, Jesus' decision, parents' confusion, search and discovery—in rapid fashion. If anything, the economy of Luke's narration heightens the sense of outrage in the reader, who knows that Jesus consciously stayed behind and forced a three-day hunt by anxious parents. And then to capitalize further on that outrage, Jesus is discovered in complete control of his destiny (in contrast to his parents), the one who deflects their worried questions with questions of his own (v. 49), impatient and devoid of concern. The cool fielding of questions in the temple (v. 47) seems to have carried over to Jesus' treatment of his own parents (v. 49).

It is as though Luke seeks to close the gap between infancy and adulthood as quickly as possible. Mark avoids the problem altogether by beginning his Gospel with the adult John and Jesus' baptism, the next episode in the Lukan presentation (3:1–22). John works in a similar direction. In the brief space of a dozen verses, Luke has placed Jesus in the temple with a power and conviction not far from Malachi's own statement from Advent 2: "And the Lord whom you seek will suddenly come to his temple . . . and who can endure the day of his coming?" (3:1–2). We are prepared for the "theophany" of Jesus as early as 2:22, and it is made clear by his parents' frequent trips to Jerusalem that this one "must be in his Father's house" (2:49), a reality ironically accomplished by the righteousness of a mother and father who here appear scorned. It is their faithful adherence to the law of the Lord that brings the twelve-year-old where he belongs

(2:39). The temple has already been the scene of much of the action in Luke's infancy chapters (Zechariah's vision in 1:18–23; Jesus' presentation in 2:22–24; Simeon's acclamation in 2:25–35; and Anna's temple service and praise in 2:36–38). We are in some sense prepared to hear Jesus' own declaration in 2:49: "How is it that you sought me? Did you not know that I must be in my Father's house?" Though they do not understand (v. 50), these things are kept in the heart (v. 51) where their significance will ultimately be revealed.

Jesus will return to Jerusalem and the temple at a later time and for a later purpose. Here he is depicted as the ideal pupil, listening and asking in turn. The description of his responses ("and they were amazed at his understanding and his answers"—that is, his "thoughtful answers") foreshadows, in the final shape of Luke's presentation, the lengthy teaching carried out by Jesus in the temple, after its cleansing (19:45—21:38). Then the Malachi announcement will receive even further validation. But even at age twelve, the Lord has come suddenly to his temple.

The Name of Jesus (January 1)

Lutheran	Roman Catholic	Episcopal	Common Lectionary
Num. 6:22–27	Num. 6:22–27	Exod. 34:1–8	Num. 6:22–27
Rom. 1:1–7 or Phil. 2:9–13	Gal. 4:4–7	Rom. 1:1–7	Gal. 4:4–7 or Phil. 2:9–13
Luke 2:21	Luke 2:16–21	Luke 2:15–21	Luke 2:15–21

FIRST LESSON: NUMBERS 6:22–27

This is a self-contained unit, only loosely related to the broader context of chap. 6, which is concerned with the special vocation of the Nazirite. The Lord here prescribes to Moses the blessing to be used by the priests (sons of Aaron). The occasion of the blessing is not specified. We hear elsewhere of blessing in the context of worship at the sanctuary (Ps. 118:26) or at dismissal from worship or sacrifice (2 Sam. 6:18). In this latter instance, David was the one to "bless the people in the name of the Lord of Hosts," thereby taking upon himself the priestly function of the sons of Aaron.

The blessing itself, compact and symmetrical, looks as though it was to be pronounced over an individual due to the consistent use throughout of the second-person singular, following the jussive (i.e., "may X bless you," *yebārekekā,* "and guard, keep you," *weyishmerekā).* However, in the framework (vv. 23, 27), the blessing is to be administered to a group ("them"; "the children of Israel"; "and I will bless them," *'abārakēm).*

The blessing is of course God's. The priests are merely the human agents who pronounce the blessing. The threefold repetition of the divine name YHWH in such short space, and the unself-conscious use of anthropomorphic attributes for God (face; countenance) drives this home. God's name is "put on them," as v. 27 explains, that "I may bless them."

The images are ones of favor and protection. The Old Testament idiom "to lift the face, countenance" (same word, *pānāw,* in vv. 25, 26) indicates personal favor and the possibility for communication between parties. Letting the face fall signals despair and possible rejection (Gen. 4:5). "Confusion of face" *(bôshet happānîm)* comes as a result of treachery against God (Dan. 9:7). When God blesses, his lifted face shines upon the one he protects.

The church fathers saw a sign of the Trinity in the threefold repetition of the divine name (YHWH) in the blessing. At its most basic level, the doctrine of the Trinity stresses the reality of full communication, within God's own self and between God and creation. Father, Son, and Holy Spirit tell us something essential about who God has shown himself to be. The notion of divine communication, outpouring love, received will, and ongoing life—all these have their specific roots in God's action with Israel. God is "trinitarian" in essence because he chooses to reveal himself so completely. In this blessing, we see the will of God to full revelation and a communication of his very self to the one blessed. The result is peace *(shālôm)*: relationship with the Lord of life and well-being.

When one speaks the name of one absent, the person is really made present in the conversation and thought and emotion of those who speak the name. The name is capable of carrying the particular identity, history, and essence of the one who bears it, with what approaches his or her totality and distinct selfhood. In the passage from Exodus (34:1–8), when the Lord passes by Moses he speaks his name and thereby says something about the fuller content of who he is. This Lord is the same Lord who has already revealed himself to Moses and Israel. The name is capable of bearing a specific identity, with a specific history, and with a purpose and a future for the one to whom it has been revealed. When we celebrate the name of Jesus, we celebrate what is forever and eternally specific about this one from Nazareth, whose name involves a specific history: life, death, resurrection, and real presence whenever the name is spoken. When we say the name, we say the person, and mean something particular and unrepeatable, yet forever available in the power of God's Holy Spirit (John 1:12).

SECOND LESSON: ROMANS 1:1–7

This opening passage from Romans ends with a blessing which is customary in the Pauline corpus: "Grace to you and peace from God our Father and the Lord Jesus Christ" (cf. 1 Cor. 1:3; 2 Cor. 1:2; Gal. 1:3; Eph. 1:2; Phil. 1:2; 2 Thess. 1:2). The bulk of the pericope is an extended introduction from Paul, necessary because this is a church that he has not visited firsthand and does not fully know. He is concerned that they know who he is. For Paul, apostle set apart (cf. Gal. 1:15), who he is involves the one who called him out and sent him. As such, his own extended introduction is an introduction to Jesus Christ and a description of the identity and credentials of the Son of God.

The Christology represented here is often termed "two-stage," by which is meant that Jesus was not designated "Son of God" in the fullest sense until his resurrection from the dead (1:4). But interestingly enough, the promises of God that find their fulfillment in Jesus are quite old, with roots in the prophets and the Scriptures of the church, the Old Testament (cf. Acts 10:43). Paul uses the term "gospel of God" *(euaggelion theou)* to describe both the promises and their target in the Son. So while one can abstract a notion of "staging," such staging belongs primarily to the realm of human perception. Seen from God's perspective, the designation Son of God may achieve its most profound application at one specific historical moment (resurrection), due to the spirit of holiness evidenced in the life and death of Jesus of Nazareth; but from the same divine perspective, this is but the final chapter in a story whose roots are ancient, involving the gospel of God "which he promised beforehand" (v. 2). If there is a qualitative distinction to be made it might be between Jesus as Son of God in humility and death and "Son of God in power" (v. 4)—not between earthly man and elevated Son of God. Moreover, the concluding blessing of grace and peace from God now of necessity involves the grace and peace of the Lord Jesus Christ (v. 7). They have been shown to be one and the same "grace and peace." Jesus is Christ (Messiah) and Lord. He is the lifted face and countenance of the divine LORD (YHWH).

Luther spoke of the preface to Romans as the essence of the Christian and evangelical faith, with which the believer could see into the heart of the Old Testament, grasping its full power and majesty. On the day when we celebrate the Holy Name of Jesus, we celebrate a grace and peace that emanates as blessing from the Father and the Son.

GOSPEL: LUKE 2:(15–)21

Luke does not, like Matthew, present a theological interpretation of the name of Jesus: "You shall call his name Jesus, for he will save his people from their sins" (Matt. 1:21). The significance of the name Jesus does not lie for Luke in the realm of etymology (about which there is some modern debate) and in the original Hebrew meaning of the name "Jesus" (Yahweh is salvation; Yahweh is help; Yahweh, Help!). Rather, what is important is the revelation of the name from heaven, given before the child was born (cf. Matt. 1:18–21), and that the act of naming takes place in obedient response to the original angelic directive: "You shall call his name Jesus" (Luke 1:31).

It has been correctly observed that much of the action in this second chapter of Luke's infancy narrative proceeds nicely with little reference to John and the contents of chapter 1. But here the link to the annunciation is made clear ("the name given by the angel before he was born"). Moreover, the reader is certainly meant to sense something of the contrast between the circumcision and naming of Jesus and the circumcision and naming of John (1:57–66). Much of the energy in the depiction of John's naming turns on the initial disbelief of Zechariah (1:20). Zechariah is mute, if not also deaf (they make signs to him at 1:62). A name is therefore proffered by those attending the circumcision. Elizabeth insists upon John, a name otherwise unknown but in wondrous congruity with the angel's announcement to her husband. This choice is confirmed by Zechariah and his tongue is loosed. This strange series of events sets off a mood of fear and puzzlement (1:65), issuing into the question: "What then will this child be?" (v. 66).

No such events attend the naming of Jesus. The story can be told in one verse. Mary was faithful to the initial vision (cf. Zechariah) and is likewise obedient here. No etymology or theologizing. The ensuing puzzlement is caused by other reasons directly related to Jesus' speech and actions (2:50).

Though there is a change of emphasis with the decision to call this day "The Holy Name of Jesus," as against the old calendar designation, "The Feast of the Circumcision," in Luke's account special interest in the name itself does not overshadow the significance of the circumcision. January 1 retains its importance because of a temporal factor: it is the eighth day, the Octave of Christmas. In accordance with the injunction given to Abraham (Gen. 21:4), Jesus, like John before him, is circumcised on the eighth day after his birth. He is marked with the "sign of the covenant" (Gen. 17:11) and made a full-fledged member of the community of faith, entitled to celebrate Passover (2:42), obliged to orient his life around God's will as specifically revealed to Israel (Gal. 4:4).

The decision to include vv. 15, 16–21 as a prelude to 2:21 in Roman Catholic and Episcopal lectionaries seems motivated by a number of factors. Reading a single verse may seem odd. But the verse, though redactional, fits better with what follows than with what precedes. Episcopalians read only 2:1–14 on Christmas Day and the Johannine Prologue (1:1–18) on the First Sunday after Christmas. This gives them the chance to hear the rest of the intervening Lukan material.

Roman Catholics are invited to reflect on Mary, mother of God, with the inclusion of vv. 15–20.

The clear occasion of the day, however, is the Circumcision of Jesus, that act of incorporation by which Jesus will effect the salvation of Israel, and the whole of humanity, consistent with the language of the prophet Isaiah. Incarnation involves a scandal of particularity, a fact driven home when Jesus is circumcised. Yet this scandal is the grounds for rejoicing, for Jesus is the particular fulfillment of particular promises shared long ago with a particular people. Only from this particular vantage point can we be made partakers with Christ in the saving life of the God of Israel, the Lord of the entire cosmos.

A brief word about some other lectionary readings, which offer their own distinctive message for this day, is in order.

The long Isaiah reading (49:1–10) stresses Israel's mission as servant (v. 3) not just to "the tribes of Jacob" and the "preserved of Israel" (v. 6), but to the nations at large "that my salvation may reach to the ends of the earth" (v. 6). This is often considered the unique message of the great Prophet of the Exile. But the streaming of the nations to Zion to worship the one Lord is a persistent theme in First Isaiah; it is in fact one of the most prominent themes running throughout the entire Isaiah corpus (2:2–3; 11:9; 19:18–25; 55:1; 56:6–8; 60:1–4).

The second lesson (Eph. 3:1–10) is chosen to develop further the theme of God's salvation to the nations, from the perspective of the apostle Paul and the early church. Paul speaks of "the mystery of Christ" (v. 4) and "the plan of the mystery hidden for ages in God who created all things" (v. 9), namely, the status of Gentiles as "fellow heirs" and partakers in the promise of God in Christ Jesus (v. 6). Such fellowship is made possible "through the gospel."

In many respects, Paul's message corresponds with the invitation of the Lukan parable in the Gospel lesson (14:16–24), an invitation issued "to many" (v. 16). God's eschatological meal, to which invitations are now being sent, is to be a full banquet, not a fast-food snack. So great is the feast that a second round of searching for guests takes place, out to the hedges and highways (v. 23). The threatening tone of the parable is meant to drive home the seriousness of the invitation being given. No one will be excluded on circumstantial grounds;

those denied access are those who were the first to get invitations, but who then decided pressing matters demanded more attention than a great eternal banquet, with "Abraham and Isaac and Jacob and all the prophets" (13:28).

The Second Sunday after Christmas

Lutheran	Roman Catholic	Episcopal	Common Lectionary
Isa. 61:10—62:3	Sir. 24:1–4, 8–12	Jer. 31:7–14	Jer. 31:7–14 or Sir. 24:1–4, 12–16
Eph. 1:3–6, 15–18	Eph. 1:3–6, 15–18	Eph. 1:3–6, 15–19a	Eph. 1:3–6, 15–18
John 1:1–18	John 1:1–18 or John 1:1–5, 9–14	Matt. 2:13–15, 19–23 or Luke 2:41–52 or Matt. 2:1–12	John 1:1–18

FIRST LESSON: ISAIAH 61:10—62:3 AND SIRACH 24:1–4, 8–12

In the latter half of the Book of Isaiah, in the sections commonly designated Second and Third Isaiah (chaps. 40–66), one sees variety in the use of first-person speech. At times, an anonymous prophet appears to speak for himself (61:1–4); at other times it is the servant who speaks (49:1–6); most often God speaks directly with the divine "I" (41:1–4). All this being said, frequently it is difficult to determine just who is speaking at what point in the text. It may also be that the notion of a sharp distinction between prophet, God, servant is misconceived.

In Isaiah 61, there is clear evidence of first-person speech from the prophet, most notably in the opening unit 61:1–4 (the lesson read by Jesus in Luke 4:18). Here the speaker sounds like one who has responded to the ideal vocation of the servant: the spirit is on him (v. 1); he speaks comfort to Zion (v. 3) and good tidings to the afflicted (v. 1). Divine speech also can be spotted in this chapter, for example, in 61:8–9.

Our pericope can be divided into two sections, 61:10–11 and 62:1–3(5). The first unit is a song of thanksgiving, not unlike what we find in the Psalter. The images here are striking. Investiture (v. 10a) and adornment (v. 10b) are familiar from Second Isaiah. They are images related to Zion/Jerusalem, or "daughter Zion," the title preferred by the prophet. So, in 49:18, the Lord promises, as a counter to the despair of Zion (49:14), that it shall put on the returning peoples "as an ornament, you shall bind them as a bride." So too, in 52:1, Zion is charged to "awake, awake . . . put on your beautiful garments!" These are the same "garments of salvation" our text refers to here; Zion as bride is a theme resumed as well in 62:4–5: "And as the bridegroom rejoices over the bride, so shall your God rejoice over you" (5b). In sum, our passage is a first-person psalm of thanksgiving, in which—not servant, nor prophet, nor God, but—Zion speaks for itself. Zion rejoices that God has made good on his promises (61:10).

In the second unit (62:1–3), critics disagree whether the prophet or God himself is the speaker. The distinction is of relative importance. The language of silence and restraint is used elsewhere in chaps. 40–66 in the context of God's own self-description (see 42:14; 64:12). Here too, God seems to speak directly. The time of silence is over: compare 42:14, "For a long time I have held my peace," and 62:1, "For Zion's sake I will not keep silence" (same Hebrew verb, *ḥšh*). Zion will now receive a new name (see 62:4; 62:12). It will be a crown of beauty (cf. 52:1) not on the head, but in the hand ("with the authority of"; "in the power of") of God, as is also the royal diadem (v. 3).

We have a sort of dialogue set up in 61:10—62:3. Zion speaks first, and God responds to confirm the exultation. They work in concert again. Zion is God's Holy Place, God's dwelling, God's tabernacle. In days of affliction, Zion became the cast-off bride, forlorn, skirts lifted above her head (Ezekiel 16). Now Zion is to "enlarge the places of her tent" (54:2) and again be the source of God's emanating blessing to all nations. On this Sunday, when the relationship between God and Jesus is fleshed out in John's Prologue as a relationship between God and Logos, Speaker and Speech, Revealer and Revealed, it is appropriate to note the images of relationship that function in the Old

Testament to describe God's intimate involvement in word and in institution with Israel and the world. The darkness could not overwhelm Zion entirely. John will turn to an even more profound exploration of darkness and light, the latter image rooted in the Word and in what is life in humanity (John 1:4–5).

Alongside Zion and the Word of God, spoken to the prophets, the Old Testament also explores God's self-revelation in the name *(shēm)* and in wisdom *(ḥochmāh)*. In Prov. 8:22–31, wisdom is depicted as one of God's "first ways" (v. 22), set up before the beginning of the earth (v. 23), in intimate fellowship with God (8:27). Our Sirach passage (24:1–4, 8–12, 13–16) adopts a similar perspective with more extended imagery. Wisdom has her origin in the mouth of the Most High (v. 3), a theme doubtless drawn from the creation account of Genesis 1, where it is God's word that creates. John will prefer this central image *(logos)* in his description of the preexistent Christ, as against wisdom *(sophia)*. In Sirach, wisdom is no longer just there with God when creation takes place (cf. Prov. 8:27–31), but can be described as taking a creative role herself: "Alone I made the vault of heaven" (v. 5). Having exercised this role, she seeks a resting place (v. 7) within the created realm (also John 1:9–13). Indeed, mention of the tent *(skēnēn mou)* assigned by God for wisdom (v. 8), as well as the establishment of a dwelling place *(kataskēnōson)* doubtless triggered John's use of similar language in the climactic v. 14: "And the word became flesh and dwelt *(eskēnōsen)* among us." Wisdom in Sirach was there at the beginning, and exists for eternity (v. 9). The final images of the strophe (vv. 10–12) tell of wisdom's lodging in Zion, among the people of Israel, a movement that is described as frustrated in John 1:11. Finally, wisdom can be depicted as Torah itself in Sir. 24:23.

In this compounding of images that seek to describe God's relationship and revelation to Israel, we have the seeds for the development of John's sublime Prologue, which relates Jesus to God, the cosmos, Israel, and believers ("we" of vv. 14, 16).

SECOND LESSON: EPHESIANS 1:3–6, 15–18

This passage was chosen for several reasons, primarily the result of its juxtaposition with the Prologue from John on this Second Sunday after Christmas. There the notion of Christ's preexistence as *logos* is set forth. Along with it, God empowers believers to become his children (John 1:12). This empowerment works on no analogy with human reproduction or other forms of biological generation (1:13); it is the result of divine fiat, a begetting that is made possible through the union of belief in Christ and God's will and self.

In Ephesians, a slightly different image is developed to talk about becoming God's children. The language used involves God's blessing *(eulogēsas ēmas)* and God's active choice *(exelexato)*, concepts closely allied with election themes and language in the Old Testament. In many respects, however, the key term here is adoption (v. 5): "he destined us in love to be his sons," or more literally, "he designated us for adoption through Christ Jesus unto him" *(eis hyiothesian)*. As distinct from John's language, Paul's use of "adoption" as a controlling image (see also Gal. 4:4–5) moves us into the realm of the juridical and the economic: believers chosen and adopted have specific rights, privileges, and inheritance. This is cause for celebration!

Now the curious thing is that Paul understands this blessing, choosing, and adopting to have occurred at God's behest "before the foundation of the world" (v. 4, *pro katabolēs kosmou*). It is one thing—rather preposterous on its own terms—to talk about the preexistence of Christ, the fellowship between God and the *logos,* the relationship between the *logos* and the cosmos, "before the foundation of the world"—quite apart from such talk about wisdom, or Torah, or the word from God's creating mouth. But how can Paul use the same language to talk about God's choosing of believers? Does the church too have a preexistent status akin to that of Christ, antedating the very creation of the world?

The answer is a qualified "yes" and the qualification is fairly major. The existence of the church is eternally derivative of Christ's existence and preexistence. Note the repetition in vv. 3–5. God blesses us "in Christ"; chooses us "in him"; adopts us as children "through Jesus Christ." Since the church's existence is fundamentally predicated on the existence of the Word, its "preexistence" is of an altogether different order. Paul is speaking here of what was forever our destiny "in Christ." Because this destiny has been extended and seized by him and present believers, it is a small leap of faithful imagination to see

God's will at work from the very first, before anything else was taken up by him in the act of creating. When the imagination is thus engaged, theology glimpses for a moment the essence of its own contemplation and becomes what it is intended to be: Doxology! Blessed be the God and Father of our Lord Jesus Christ who has blessed us in Christ with every spiritual blessing! The qualitative importance of what it means to have been claimed by God, made by adoption to be God's own children, slides now into a temporal mode: God willed our adoption from the beginning because he willed Christ. Jesus is Son of God by nature and for all eternity; we are made sons and daughters by adoption. Both involve an eternal design effected within the temporal realm, "a plan for the fulness of time, to unite all things in him, things in heaven and things on earth" (1:10).

GOSPEL: JOHN 1:1–18

One critical question has engaged sensitive readers of John's Prologue: At what point in the narrative (poetic) sequence does talk of the preexistent Logos end and the incarnate Logos begin? One might hope to take guidance from the pivotal v. 14, "And the Word became flesh and dwelt among us," which reading would then involve seeing all that precedes as a description of the Word (true light) coming into the world prior to Christmas, in Israel (his own people) and the larger world.

Mention of John in v. 6 tends, however, to prepare the reader for the frustration (v. 11) and success (vv. 12–13) associated with the drama of the Word in the world, in earthly dress, in the life and mission of Jesus. But the mention of John at this point cannot force such an interpretation. Verses 6–8 are clearly on the order of a footnote, explaining that the light of v. 5 is not John but Jesus. Critics have rightly viewed this note as provided by the actual author of the Gospel, especially if an original hymn lies behind the prologue, inherited by John, having its point of origin in early Christian assembly. This note would then serve not just to clarify the light of v. 5, but also would more tightly link the Prologue with the Gospel proper—in which discussion of John's role vis-à-vis Jesus does ensue (see 3:22–30). The status of the verse as an explanatory note, whose placement is simply occasioned by the reference to the light in v. 5, could permit the reader to move on to vv. 9–13 and hear of the experience of the Word in the world, and in Israel, prior to the incarnation. Such was the drift of the Sirach passage, where wisdom took up lodging "in Zion," "in the portion of the Lord." Clearly the Old Testament knows as well of the rejection of wisdom in Israel, and the refusal of Israel to heed the Word of God spoken through the prophets. Such is the force of the prologue's depiction of the fate of the Word in the world.

Fortunately, it is probably not necessary to cast all votes in one direction or the other. At a minimum, the reader will hear in these lines a resonance of the experience of the Logos in the world before the incarnation occurred. This may have been clearer in the original form of the hymn. Verses 1–5 tell of the relationship between the Word and God and the Word and creation; vv. 9–13 tell of the Word's checkered history, favorably received by only a portion; vv. 14, 16–18 relate the Word's becoming flesh, the beholding of glory, and the gifts of grace and truth "through Jesus Christ." There is a nice, episodic quality captured in this staging of the narrative. At the same time, it is difficult to hear vv. 9–13, especially the references to becoming God's children (see 3:1–21) and the light in the world (3:19) without drawing the whole ensuing story of the incarnate Jesus into consciousness. The final effect is like that of three concentric circles. The light in the experience of Israel and the world, in the incarnate Jesus, and in the present age's reception or nonreception of the Word—all three worlds have their center in the eternal will of God expressed in the Word. The experience of one circle anticipates the experience of another.

The riches of this text are inexhaustible. One has the sense that every word matters, that the rough edges have been worn down by use and reuse, if not trial and error. Every word matters and other words could not fill the space these occupy, in this or any other configuration. Only a line-by-line exposition can begin to chart out something of the compact genius of this eighteen-verse hymn. In many respects, everything is here. What follows in the Gospel of John is simply an illustration of details of truth to which this hymn points.

In this Advent/Christmas season, we have looked far down the landscape of the biblical world to catch the language of hope and conviction about the coming one and the just ruler straining for fulfillment. We have also seen resurrection faith in Jesus the Son of God transferred from a single historical moment, following the death and resurrection, to the event of Nativity itself on the one hand and the end of the ages on the other. The voice from heaven identifies this one even before the birth: "He will be the Son of the Most High" (Luke 1:32). Backward and forward in time, all lines intersect in Jesus of Nazareth. Having fastened in scandalously particular fashion the hopes of the ages on this child, having said it happened in the birth so surely as in the death, John takes the truth of this movement yet one step further. In this sharply chiseled Prologue we see what is the only possible next word about Jesus, and at the same time, the last word about Jesus, the final truth: "In the beginning was the Word and the Word was with God and the Word was God." It has been said. We know about the Word of God, revealed to Israel by the prophets, etched on the pages of Scripture. Now we confront the "Word was God," the Word, *o logos*. The eternal Word takes flesh and raises for us the eternal question: Shall we receive him? As Advent gives way to Christmas, and Christmas to Epiphany, we begin to see the question posed as sharply as ever, in the language of John's realized eschatology: "This is the judgment, that the light has come into the world . . . " (3:19). The preparation for the second coming of advent has turned our eyes back to the first coming, a coming with which we must now contend in order to be given "power to become the children of God" (John 1:13) in this and every age.

During this Advent/Christmas season, we have seen the stage set and the actors coming into view one by one: Isaiah, Jeremiah, Samuel, Malachi, Zechariah, Elizabeth, Joseph, Mary, and John. Now the main actor appears and we learn he has written the play. Then we learn that the play is about us. Suddenly we too are on stage and there is no longer a division between actor and audience, player and viewer. The script sounds like the life we know but also very unlike the life we know, for the main actor who acts there with us seems to sense the full story and knows its end and ours. It is now difficult, no, impossible, to return to our seats. "Do you want to go away?" he will shortly ask (6:67). For those who have beheld his glory, Peter's simple answer

masks a whole range of emotions: "To whom shall we go? You have
the words of eternal life" (6:68). Advent has given way to Christmas,
and Christmas to Epiphany. There is a kind of sure judgment in this
light, and John has captured it well. The Word has become flesh, and
dwelt among us, and we have beheld its glory, "glory as of the only
Son from the Father" (1:14). But then the Prologue points to the end
of the story, where the ultimate gift of following this one, of staying
on this stage and with this script, is made clear: "And from his fulness
have we all received, grace upon grace" (1:16). With this final word
from John's Prologue, we move squarely into the Epiphany season,
which moves beyond the birth to celebrate the dwelling of the Word
among us.